If They're Laughing, They're Not Killing Each Other

Ideas for using humor effectively in the classroom — even if you're not funny yourself

Elaine M. Lundberg
and
Cheryl Miller Thurston

Illustrated by Patricia Howard

Cottonwood Press, Inc.
Fort Collins, Colorado

Requests for permission should be addressed to:

Cottonwood Press, Inc.
305 West Magnolia, Suite 398
Fort Collins, CO 80521

ISBN 1-877673-14-5

Printed in the United States of America

The authors would like to thank the following for permission to use copyrighted material.

Excerpt from "The Other Funny Thing in the Classroom . . . Kids," by Benny Hickerson, *English Journal*, March, 1989.

"Dinner Drama," by Jill Sverdlove, *Denver Post* (Contemporary), June 28, 1992.

Excerpts from the *Cottonwood Monthly, Did You Really Fall into a Vat of Anchovies?, Extra Book Level 2, Mystery of the Suffocated Seventh Grader, Ideas that Really Work!* and *Hide Your Ex-Lax Under the Wheaties*, all published by Cottonwood Press, Inc.

Acknowledgments

The authors would like to thank the following people for their help in completing this book:

- David Lundberg-Kenrick, for laughing at Elaine's jokes, even though she is his mom.

- Ed Armstrong, for putting up with not one but two redheads in the house during Elaine's trips to Colorado to work on the book, and for marrying Cheri anyway.

- United Airlines, for frequent flyer miles.

- Kathy Dewhirst, Dawn DiPrince, Rory Franklin, Judy Porter Reid, Patsy Shouse and Amy Zesbaugh for their valuable and varied assistance in putting this book together.

- Our fathers, John Miller and Vincent Wilhelmson, for giving us each, separately of course, a healthy sense of humor.

Table of Contents

Please note: All activities marked with a star (★) may be photocopied for the purchaser's own personal use in his or her own school, classes or workshops.

Introduction

"If they're laughing, they're not killing each other" is a philosophy that applies to people in general and also to students in a classroom. A classroom filled with laughter is a classroom with positive energy. It is a classroom where students feel free to use their creativity to its fullest; where time is spent building up, rather than tearing down; where students feel free to try, to fail and to grow, without fear. We believe, in fact, that if they're laughing, they're probably learning, too.

The positive energy generated by laughter in a classroom does not end with the students. There is a phenomenon we like to call the "Pregnant Woman Syndrome." If you have ever been pregnant, you probably remember noticing, once you heard the news, how many pregnant women there are in the world. (Similarly, if you started going bald, you probably started noticing bald men all over the place. Or if you bought a new Honda Accord, you started seeing Honda Accords everywhere.) The Pregnant Woman Syndrome also applies to humor. Once you start thinking about humor and incorporating more of it in your classroom, ideas for humor will leap out at you all the time. You will start to find yourself using your own creativity and abilities to the fullest extent, and enjoying yourself more.

And that will probably help you become even more effective as a teacher.

A word of caution: Humor is very personal. What individuals find humorous varies greatly from one person to another — so much so, in fact, that it often amazes us. We don't expect you to find every story in this book amusing, or to see every idea as one you could use in your classroom. Take what you can use, and leave the rest.

We hope this book will make you think about humor in your own classroom — about its importance and about new ways to use it with your students. We hope you will believe, as we do, that with laughter, learning can flourish.

Why should humor and laughter be a part of every classroom?

No matter what your teaching style, humor can be an important addition to your classroom. Used in various forms and to various degrees, humor enriches any learning environment. Here are a number of reasons why:

Humor makes class more interesting. Students can't learn anything if they aren't paying attention. Humor relieves monotony and boredom and helps students stay tuned in, keeping their attention so that they can learn. If they know something funny might happen at any moment, they listen. When they listen, the teacher is more effective.

With older students, humor is even more of a motivator. It helps bring students to class, and it keeps them coming back.

> **"The job of the teacher is to get students laughing, and when their mouths are open, to give them something on which to chew."**
>
> **Tom Davis**

Humor helps both students and teacher enjoy class more. Some people act as though real learning takes place only if there is suffering involved. Nonsense. People who enjoy class are more likely to be motivated. Similarly, teachers who enjoy what they do are more likely to be effective at what they do. One of the greatest benefits of humor is to enhance the teacher's enjoyment of class. Humor can help a teacher remain fresh, interesting and on his or her toes.

Laughter reduces tension and anxiety. Humor disarms. It can be used to diffuse awkward, tense or even ugly situations in the classroom. It's hard to laugh and be angry at the same time.

Humor can help students learn to deal with hostile and aggressive feelings. It reduces tension and anxiety, helping students to relax so that they are able to learn. It is also useful in helping teachers deal with the stresses and demands of teaching. Laugher makes them better — and saner — teachers.

Humor motivates and energizes. When a teacher creates a learning environment where humor is welcome and even encouraged, students often try harder. There is a positive feeling in such a classroom. There is an energy that is both stimulating and infectious.

Humor gives students a "hook" on which to trigger recall. When we learn, we link new information with old information. We relate the new to something we already know, in order to fit it into our world and make sense of it. Humor can help us make that link. For example, when science students remember a cartoon from class about Einstein and the theory of relativity, they are making a connection that will help them recall what they studied in class about relativity. The cartoon is the "hook" for recall.

Humor encourages creativity. Creativity and humor are close relatives. Recent studies show that a humorous atmosphere significantly increases students' creativity scores. Because humor often comes from the unexpected, it surprises us with a new perspective, giving us new ways of looking at familiar objects and events. It shakes us up and opens our minds, freeing our thoughts, making us less focused on "rules" and "the right way" and "the correct answer."

Humor helps students accept new ideas. New ideas are often threatening to us. They disturb our world, forcing us to question our views. Humor can make new ideas less threatening.

For example, the threat of AIDS has made information about using condoms important for both young people and adults. To show how a condom is used properly, some instructors fit a condom over a banana. The resulting laughter helps people get past the awkwardness of the subject matter, allowing them to relax and open themselves up to receiving the information presented.

> **"It is really difficult for a student or colleague to turn off and become hostile when they are regularly enjoying a good laugh or chuckle with their teacher/leader."**
>
> **Peter Warnock**

Laughter helps build relationships.
Laughter brings people together, both physically and psychologically. It fosters friendship, bonding and building. It promotes positive feelings and a sense of belonging. When you have laughed with someone, you tend to feel a connection to that person.

Laughter helps show that mistakes are a normal part of learning.
When teachers laugh at their own mistakes, they show students that mistakes are not the end of the world. A teacher's sense of humor can help students put their own mistakes into perspective.

Humor provokes thought.
Sometimes humor makes us work. When others are laughing and we don't get the joke, we are forced to think, to look at the subject from different angles. In the classroom, a joke or a humorous situation can force students to make connections they might otherwise miss.

Laughter improves health, for both students and teachers.
More and more evidence suggests that laughter reduces stress, and that stress reduction is an important element in good health. Like it or not, we live in a world full of pressures, and reducing the effects of those pressures is helpful both in and out of the classroom, for students and teachers alike. Psychologically, a good laugh is a great way to relax and a positive tool for stress management. It releases tension and helps us triumph over life's little traumas.

When you laugh, many wonderful, healthy things go on in your body. Physiologically, you take in more oxygen; your blood pressure goes down; and your heart rate goes up. According to Dr. William Fry of Stanford Medical School, 20 seconds of belly laughing equals three minutes of hard rowing on a rowing machine. Your body also releases catacholamines, endorphins and enkephalines, which are natural pain relievers. The tears of laughter contain a natural immune substance, dlysozyme, which fights viruses in the body.

If you are interested in additional information, two good resources are *Anatomy of an Illness*, by Norman Cousins (Bantam Books, 1979) and *The Healing Power of Humor*, by Allen Klein (Tarcher, Inc., 1989).

Everyone appreciates a sense of humor.
Because a sense of humor is seen as a desirable personality trait in nearly every aspect of life, it is a quality that should be nurtured in the classroom. We encourage talent in art, sports, academics, music, etc. Perhaps we ought to do more to encourage those with a talent for making others laugh.

Laughter feels good.
Laughter gives us pleasure. We should appreciate it, welcome it, and encourage it in our lives —for no other reason than that it feels good!

Disadvantages of using humor in the classroom

Yes, there are disadvantages to using humor in the classroom. It is important to be aware of them so that you aren't surprised by them if they come up. Here are several areas of possible concern:

- Students often think of *serious* and *humorous* as mutually exclusive terms. They need to learn that school work can be humorous and serious at the same time. When there is a lot of laughter in a classroom, students sometimes think they aren't really working or learning. Other teachers may have the same attitude. If there are a lot of smiles, they assume that no work is getting done.

  Sometimes it helps to address the issue head on. Point out to students, frequently, that learning can be fun. Remind them that every class activity has a serious point, even if there is a lot of laughter involved. Have them summarize or restate the point behind every lesson.

"To be wildly enthusiastic, or deadly serious — both are wrong . . . But the sense of humor I have found of use in every single occasion of my life."

Katherine Mansfield

With colleagues, it helps to speak up about your students' successes. Without bragging, show enthusiasm about how well your students did on their last vocabulary test, and mention that you think that assignment they were laughing about had something to do with their performance. Share stories of laughter in your classroom, and always take care to mention what was behind it all — the point of the lesson. Focus on your students' accomplishments, rather than on your own technique.

No, such methods won't solve all your problems, but they may help. Let it be known at every turn that there is serious learning going on in your classroom.

- Some students may not understand the difference between positive and negative humor. If they don't, help them out. Positive humor is nurturing and kind, enhancing self-esteem. Negative humor is cutting and hurts people's feelings.

- Students sometimes look at laughter as a signal to get out of hand. Or they may lose control easily when a highly structured environment becomes more relaxed. You may need to guide students in learning that there are boundaries with humor just as there are with anything else. It is usually effective to say something like this: "If you can't get yourselves under control, we'll have to run a more serious classroom," or "You need to settle down and get back on task; otherwise you will be showing me I'd better take a more serious approach next time." Peer pressure will also help redirect any students who have a hard time catching on.

  We teach students how to behave in so many other areas of life; it should not be surprising that we need to teach them how to behave sensibly with humor, as well. They can easily learn that laughter and learning can work together, side by side.

Guidelines for using humor in the classroom

- **Don't try too hard.** Let humor arise naturally, or encourage it, but don't force it. Nothing is more painful to experience than someone trying hard to be funny — and failing.

- **Do what fits you and your personality.** Some of the ideas included in this book are ones that some of us would never dream of trying — and rightly so. Yet other teachers will use the same ideas with great success. We all have to do what fits our personalities. While we should be willing to stretch ourselves a bit, it is not a good idea to try something that is absolutely foreign to our nature.

- **Don't use private humor or humor that leaves people out.** It is rude to use humor that relies on private information that is not accessible to everyone in a group. A student should never have to be part of the "in" crowd to understand the humor of a situation in the classroom.

- **Never use humor to hurt someone, or to put someone down.** Humor that is used to hurt or demean is never suitable for the classroom — or for anywhere else. Teachers should skip stories with ethnic, racial or sexual stereotypes.

- **Make humor a regular part of class, rather than something special.** Humor works best as a natural, ongoing part of class. If you suddenly decide to do a "humor in literature" unit or a "funny math problems" unit, you may find the humor forced or strained. Humor needs a more welcoming, nurturing environment — an environment that consistently appreciates the importance of what makes us smile.

- **Tie humor to the subject you are teaching.** Whenever possible, make humor a part of your lesson, rather than something unrelated to the subject at hand. Humor can sometimes be distracting when it bears no natural relationship to what the students are studying.

E PLURIBUS UNUM

UNFORTUNATELY, MR. JONES,
THE LATIN TEACHER, ONLY
SKIMMED THIS CHAPTER.

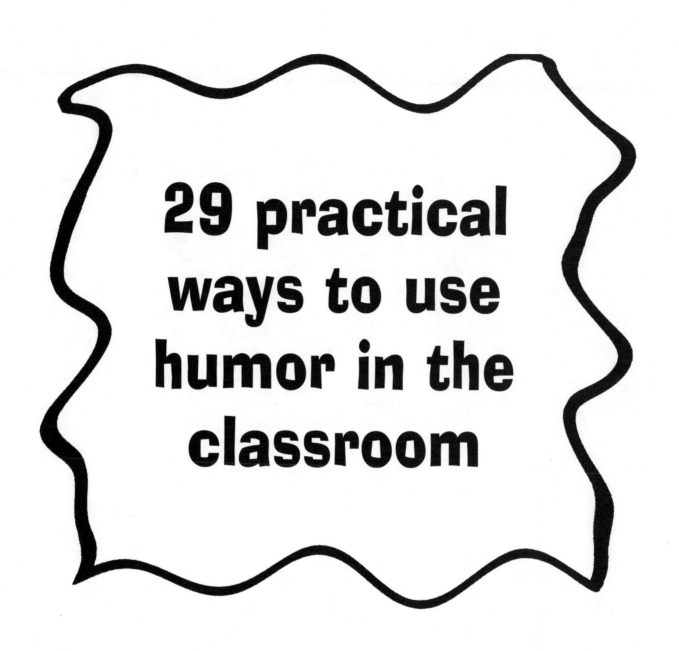

29 practical ways to use humor in the classroom

She's a little off-the-wall

Setting a tone has its advantages. Somber music at a funeral lets us know that goofing around or giggling is not appropriate. Low lights and quiet music in a cozy restaurant let us know that romance is welcome. Picnic tables and peanut shells on the floor of a bar let us know that shorts and t-shirts are suitable attire.

Similarly, the classroom itself can set a tone. If you want students to feel happy, creative and free to explore their minds and imaginations, follow this tip:

Create an environment that welcomes humor.

Make your classroom one that, physically, welcomes humor. Put up a bulletin board with jokes and cartoons. Start a "weird items" corner with amusing bumper stickers, funny headlines from the newspaper, silly wind-up animals, Halloween masks, whatever strikes your fancy.

> **"Laughter is the shortest distance between two people."**
> **Victor Borge**

One teacher we know used to pack his classroom with oddball items. Every square inch of the room that wasn't occupied by desks and books was covered with this "junk" he had been collecting for over 20 years. The items included his own drawings and cartoons, caricatures of students, an old Coke dispenser, a huge wooden bald eagle and the head end part of a mule costume. No one could enter his

room and expect it to be a dull, dry place for learning. Students knew at a glance that a sense of humor was welcome here.

For an easy bulletin board that will draw a few smiles, simply cover the board with white paper. Then put huge black letters across the middle of the board, spelling out "Generic Bulletin Board." Use the leftover space for tacking up announcements, jokes, trivia, whatever seems appropriate. The Generic Bulletin Board part can stay up all year, but you can constantly update the rest of the items.

Holiday Fun

Many of us use holidays as the focus of special lessons or activities in our classrooms. Instead of relying on just the ordinary ones — Thanksgiving, Halloween, Valentine's Day, etc. — try building lessons and activities around other special days. Below are some suggestions to get you started. Most of them are taken from *Celebrate Today!* (Open Horizons Publishing Company, 1995).

January
National Oatmeal Month

January 28
National Kazoo Day

February
National Blah Buster Month

February (fourth Friday)
French Fry Friday

March
Foot Health Month

March 1
National Pig Day

April
National Reading a Road Map Month

April 15
Rubber Eraser Day

May
National Asparagus Day

May 10–16
National Hamburger Week

June
Zoo and Aquarium Month

June 7–13
Teacher Thank You Week

July 27
Bugs Bunny's Birthday

July 30
Comedy Celebration Day

August (first week)
National Smile Week

August 20
Sit Back and Relax Day

September 22
Fantasies Are Fabulous Day

September 30
Ask a Stupid Question Day

October
National Pizza Month

October 15
National Grouch Day

November 4
Peanut Butter Lover's Day

November 6–12
National Split Pea Soup Week

December 15
Underdog Day

December 22
Look on the Bright Side Day

FOOT HEALTH MONTH

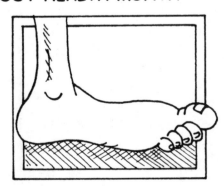

That's quite a pig!

A visitor noticed an unusual pig at a farmer's home. The pig had two wooden legs, and it roamed freely throughout the farmer's house. When the visitor commented, the farmer said, "Yes, that's quite a pig. We had a fire a couple of month ago, and that pig butted its head against the door, ran into the house, and went room to room waking every family member."

"Wow!" said the visitor, impressed. "But why does the pig have two wooden legs?"

"Well, just last week the tractor started to roll over me, and this pig pulled me out from under it and saved my life!"

"Yes, yes," said the visitor. "But WHY does he have two wooden legs?"

"Good heavens," said the farmer, shocked. "You can't eat a good pig like that all at *once!*"

Who knows when you will be able to use an old joke like this in the classroom? That's why it's a good idea to adopt the following idea:

Keep your own "humor therapy" log.

Start now keeping a file of funny items. Include amusing things your students have said or done in the class. Include jokes, cartoons, quips, stories, funny newspaper articles, quirky facts, trivia, etc. — all related to your subject, to your school, to learning, to life in general or to nothing in particular. You can then take a look at the book when preparing tests, handouts, transparencies, lessons or other materials — or perhaps just when you need a lift or a reminder that all is not as grim as it seems.

You don't need to have a purpose in mind for the items you collect. Cheryl Thurston, for example, once heard a story she loved about a rabbit. (Of course, when she heard it, the story was supposedly true, but who knows?) She filed the story away. Months later, when she needed a proofreading exercise, she simply rewrote the story purposely misspelling 100 words. The resulting assignment follows (page 18).

> **"So long as there's a bit of a laugh going, things are all right. As soon as this infernal seriousness, like a greasy sea, heaves up, everything is lost."**
>
> **D.H. Lawrence**

★ Tail of a dead rabit

(with 100 spelling errors)

Once upon a time, a teanager named Ann lived with her dog Henry in a charming littel howse in the suberbs. Next too her lived a littel gril named Marie, who razed rabits in her bakyard. She had at leest forteen rabits living in huches. They're were rabits of all collars, including grey, black, wite and brown. Marie's favrite was a spoted rabit named Georgie. She liked him becaus he was so clever and had so mutch engerny.

One day Ann was siting on her patio reeding a book called *The Imposible Dreem.* As she relacksed with the deliteful love story, her dog Henry sudenly bounded into the yard.

"How did you get out?" cryed Ann. She didn't like for Henry too run lose, for the dogcacher would pick him up and give Ann a fine. "Their is no exkuse for this!" she scowlded Henry. "You must not go out of this yard."

Then Ann looked down and saw that Henry was carring somthing. It was a rabit, a dead rabit. Furthemore, it was the spoted rabit named Georgie.

"How could you do such a thing?" said Ann. "How could you kill Georgie?" She began sobing as she remuved the dirtey aminal from the dog's mouth. "Marie will kill me. This is her favrite rabit. She will feel terible."

Serching carfuley, Ann saw that they're were no cuts on the rabit, just alot of mud. She thought for a minite. Then she took the dead rabit to the fawcett and began carfully washing it off, removeing all the dirt and mud. "This may not be very honest," thoght Ann, "but I feal it is necesary. I don't want Marie two no this is Henry's fault."

She waited until Marie left for her danse leson. Then she sneeked into her yard, opened a cage, and placed the dead rabit Georgie back inside. "Now she will never no," sighed Ann. "She won't blame Henry, and she won't blame me," She was very sory the rabit was dead, but she didn't want Marie too be angry with her. Marie had a terible temper.

That night Ann was lieing on the sofa watching tevelision when the doorbell wrang. She opened the door.

"It's incredibul!" cried Marie.

"What is?" replyed Ann. "Clam down."

"I new that the bunnie named Georgie had engerny, but I never, ever thought. . ."

"Though what?"

"Well, Georgie dyed yesterday," said Marie. "I don't know what happened to him, but he dyed. Natchrally, I felt awfel, but buryed him out back behind my back fence. Then this evning, when I went to fead the rabits, their was Georgie again — back in the cage! He was still dead, of course, but he had unberried himself and fownd his way back into the cage with his brothers and sisters! It's amasing!"

"Yes," said Ann slowley. "It's amasing. Come sit down a minute, Marie. I've got some explaning too do."

Reprinted from *Extra Book, Level 2* (Cottonwood Press, Inc.)

Sometimes teachers can use a shot of humor therapy. Perhaps this test can help you or your colleagues.

★ Teacher stress test

Stress is, unfortunately, a normal part of the job for most teachers. However, too much stress can be dangerous to a person's health and well-being. Check out your level of stress by marking all the following items that apply to you:

_____   You have disruptive kids in your classroom.

_____   You have disruptive kids in your home.

_____   You have mainstreamed kids in your classroom.

_____   The water main broke and streamed into your classroom.

_____   Your principal hates you.

_____   You hate your principal.

_____   Your students hate you.

_____   You have gifted students in your classroom.

_____   You have gifted students in your classroom, and you are afraid some of
_____   them might be smarter than you.

_____   You have been transferred to a new school.

_____   You can't find your new school.

_____   You have been given a different classroom.

_____   You can't find your new classroom.

_____   Your new classroom is a converted boiler room.

_____   Your department head is an idiot.

_____   Your department head is dating the principal.

_____   Violence is a problem in your school or classroom.

_____   Violence is a problem in the teachers' lounge.

_____   You have bus duty.

_____   You have lunch duty.

_____   You have recess duty.

_____   You have bus duty, lunch duty and recess duty all on the same day.

_____   You have more than 25 kids in a class.

_____   You have more than 25 kids in a class, and only 22 desks.

_____   Teachers in your district are talking about going on strike.

_____   Teachers in your district *are* on strike.

_____   You refuse to take part in the strike.

_____   The teachers on strike hate you.

(continued)

(continued)

_____	You are having problems with some parents.
_____	You are having problems with your own parents.
_____	You are having problems being a parent.
_____	You received no salary increase this year.
_____	You will receive no salary increase next year.
_____	Your contract was not renewed, so you will have no salary next year.
_____	You have to go to the office to use a telephone at school.
_____	You have to get permission to call long distance.
_____	Your therapist's office is long distance.
_____	You coach one or more athletic activities.
_____	Your teams have never won a game.
_____	You are taking classes at night to move up on the pay scale.
_____	You sometimes fantasize about becoming a waitress or a welder.
_____	You have no planning period.
_____	You have no planning, period.
_____	You missed your last period.
_____	You didn't plan, period.
_____	You aren't married.
_____	You have an appointment at Family Planning, during lunch period.
_____	You get only 28 minutes for lunch.
_____	You forgot your lunch and have to eat the cafeteria's Spanish rice.
_____	You lose your lunch.
_____	The principal tells you you have a call from Family Planning.

Scoring

Give yourself one point for every item you checked.

0–10 points:	You are lying.
15–25 points:	Your stress level falls within the normal range for most teachers.
26–39 points:	You could explode at any moment. Be sure your family is insured.
Over 40 points:	Take a deep breath. Sit down. Call 911 immediately.

Quaker chuckles and zany Buddhist humor

In at least one library in this country, there is a book called *Quaker Chuckles*. For some reason, we found the title very funny and couldn't resist checking out the book. It turns out that the title is a lot funnier than the book. A lot funnier. Still, it brings to mind many possible book titles — perhaps *Zany Buddhist Humor, Cackles from the Convent, Methodist Mirth* or *Those Wacky Amish.*

Perhaps you don't find a title like *Quaker Chuckles* at all amusing. That's all right. What is it you *do* find funny? Make your own choices in order to do the following:

Begin class each day with something humorous.

It's easy to get students' attention, and to set a positive tone for class, by beginning each day with a humorous quotation, joke or cartoon. Use the overhead projector or the chalk board, and students will soon get into the habit of looking for your daily item. Students themselves will start bringing in jokes to contribute, and you will probably find it easy to get material for

> **"Humor is the great thing, the saving thing, after all. The minute it crops up, all our hardnesses yield, all our irritations and resentments slip away, and a sunny spirit takes their place."**
>
> **Mark Twain**

your daily "offering." Keep an eye out for possible items, and keep them in a file. It's a good idea to mark each item as you use it, for it is very easy to forget what you have used after you have been doing your joke-a-day items for a month or so.

It's nice when humorous items relate to your discipline or to the unit you are teaching, but don't limit your selections to such items. Use whatever you find amusing, and don't worry if the students don't appreciate your sense of humor. In a good-natured way, persist with your selections, but invite them to share their own.

One of the benefits of beginning class with something humorous is that you start class on a positive note. Also, while students are not usually eager to quiet down and start studying when then come into class, they are likely to quiet down in order to see or hear something funny. Reward them for paying attention by including bonus questions on tests about some of the humorous items you have used at the beginning of class.

The items can be as varied as you like. Here are some samples from one teacher's beginning-of-class repertoire:

- Why wouldn't the King Potato and the Queen Potato let the Princess Potato marry Walter Cronkite? Because he was only a common 'tator.

- What do you see in this picture?

Possible answer: A mosquito showing off his latest work.

- Why don't cannibals eat clowns? Because they taste funny.

- What did one earthquake say to another? It's not my fault.

- What happens to a ghost when he falls down on the sidewalk? He gets a boo-boo.

- How do you tell when an elephant has been in your refrigerator? There are footprints in the Jell-O.

- If a plane crashes exactly on the border between Canada and the United States, where do they bury the survivors? You don't bury survivors!

After you have started class with something funny every day for a year or so, you may have enough items to make your own personal joke-a-day calendar or a booklet of your favorite items. You might even use the calendar or booklets as prizes at your own end-of-the-year classroom awards ceremonies, just for the fun of it.

Trademarks

A teacher we know collects buttons, everything from political buttons to buttons with ridiculous sayings or cartoons. He has made the buttons his trademark, and he wears a different one every day. Everyone at school is always eager to see what he is wearing, and they also contribute amusing buttons they have found to his collection.

Any teacher can develop a trademark. For example he or she might wear outrageous socks, wild earrings, funny T-shirts, unusual ties. Or the teacher might collect unusual coffee mugs, Calvin and Hobbes cartoons, cow knickknacks or ceramic penguins. If it fits you, a trademark can add a bit of fun to your classroom.

What's happening, baby?

Think back to your own childhood. What do you remember best — things that you read about, things that you heard about or things that you did? For most of us, our strongest memories involve things that we did. Active involvement encourages remembering and learning, and it also allows humor to emerge naturally. So — remember this tip when you are planning lessons:

Use activities, activities, activities!

Activities are effective tools for learning, and they can vary widely. They can range from extremely simple (like having students work problems on the board) to the fairly complex (like having them create skits or plays that illustrate a principle). Whatever the activity, humor is often an enjoyable by-product, even if the activity itself is not humorous.

> **"He who laughs, lasts."**
> **Mary Pettibone Poole**

For example, one teacher of senior adults has her students construct a floor plan of their childhood homes in order to help them recall memories of childhood. They are encouraged to draw in rooms, major pieces of furniture and outside structures like barns, outhouses, fences or fire escapes. They are asked, as they draw, to think about what they used to see, think, hear, feel, touch and smell in that house when they were growing up. The memories always start flooding in, and the students begin to share.

Laughter is always involved as students remember humorous stories from their childhoods. Is the activity itself humorous? No. Does it generate smiles and laughter and pleasant memories? Most definitely.

Twenty ways to smile or laugh

Chuckle, roar, grin, smile, smirk, chortle, beam, break up, howl, cackle, guffaw, roar, roll in the aisles, crack up, snicker, be in stitches, titter, giggle, snort, shriek.

Did you really fall into a vat of anchovies? (below) is an activity that can be used with adults and children alike. Because it is a good ice breaker, it is perfect for the first day or two of a workshop or class, and it will usually generate some very funny responses. It is also interesting to use at the end of the school year or at the end of a workshop, when people think they know one another pretty well. The results will often surprise the participants.

★ Did you really fall into a vat of anchovies?
or
Using little-known personal facts
for fascinating classroom exploration

A student once told me that, as a child, she had fallen into a vat of anchovies in San Francisco. So I told her about the dimple I have, made by a screen door hook that caught in my open mouth and poked itself all the way through my cheek. Then I told her about my childhood school bus driver who later wound up on the FBI's Ten Most Wanted list. (I probably didn't mention that I had a crush on him. How was I to know he was going to turn out to be a criminal?)

Such oddball facts fill all of our lives, though we may not be able to recall them at a moment's notice. Recalling them, however, can have a lot of possibilities for the classroom. Follow the directions below and see what develops. You are likely to hear some fascinating tales, laugh a lot and make some interesting discoveries.

Directions

Ask your students to brainstorm facts about themselves, facts that others might be surprised to know about them. The facts can be trivial or important, funny or serious. Ask them not to share their facts with one another as they brainstorm.

Of course, it may be hard to come up with unusual facts without a bit of thought. Suggest that students think about the following areas: places they have visited or lived; things they love; things they hate; people they have met or known; something they wish or long for; awards they have won; unusual injuries they have received; sights they have witnessed; misfortunes they have overcome; and unusual facts about relatives, ancestors or friends.
After they have brainstormed for a while, give them this assignment:

List five facts that you are willing to share about yourself, facts that you think are unknown to most of the class. However, there is a catch: One of the "facts" must be a lie. (Don't worry; the lies are only temporary. The class will try to guess which of your "facts" isn't really true.)

It's a good idea to give students time to think about the assignment, writing up their lists for homework and perhaps enlisting the help of family members. You might also suggest that students base their temporary lies on something that is true — but about someone else. For example, I told one class that I met my husband because of a high school letter jacket from Afghanistan. I was attending a dance in America, I said, and saw a young man wearing a letter jacket from the high school I had attended in Afghanistan, where my father was stationed. I introduced myself and found out that we had attended the same school, but at different times.

We got to talking; one thing led to another; and eventually we wound up husband and wife.

The story is not true about me, but it is true about a woman I know. Remind your students that truth often really *is* stranger than fiction.

If students need some examples to get them thinking, you might share these facts written by one student:

- I rode my first snowmobile at the age of one month.
- My stepfather once walked on the Great Wall of China.
- I traveled through Germany at age seven with my father's girlfriend's 68-year-old mother and her granddaughter.
- I was once a junior rodeo queen at the Bonneville Stampede in Idaho.
- A navy lieutenant once interviewed me as the only eyewitness to a terrible collision between two navy vehicles in Washington.

(The lie: being a junior rodeo queen.)

Here are the facts from another student:

- My hard-of-hearing grandfather has ten telephones in his house, all connected to lights that go off when the phone rings.
- For six months, I had a pet tarantula named Boris.
- Because of a friend's "joke," there was once a rumor all over my home town that I had committed suicide.
- I was once in a Taos bookstore at the same time as Arnold Schwarzenegger and Maria Shriver.
- Once while in the attic, my dad fell through on my visiting aunt's head. She left soon after.

(The lie: having a pet tarantula.)

After all the students — and you, too — have listed their "facts," have them get into small groups to share their lists and to have others guess which of their "facts" are really lies. Many of the facts will have stories behind them, and students will want to hear the stories. When the class gets back together, ask groups to share some of the more interesting stories. Better yet, if your class is small enough, have each student share his or her "facts" with the whole class.

Finally, have your students discuss their reactions to the assignment, orally or in writing. What surprised them? What did they learn? What generalities can they make? Are there any lessons to be learned from the activity? (The questions make a perfect subject for exploration in student journals.) You might also ask each student to write the story behind one of his or her "facts." (How did it come about? Why? What were the circumstances?)

It's also fun to type up a list of facts (the true ones!) about the students to share with students themselves, other teachers and/or parents.

Cheryl Miller Thurston

Reprinted from *Did You Really Fall into a Vat of Anchovies — and other activities for Language Arts* (Cottonwood Press, Inc.)

There's life after chocolate

When teachers think of rewards for their students, they usually think of candy, especially if their students are relatively young. However, there are so many more possibilities, no matter what the age of your students. An easy way to add spice to your classroom is to follow this tip:

Give silly awards.

People of any age love recognition. Recognition, however, doesn't have to be in the form of a valuable prize or a fancy trophy. Use your imagination for some unusual rewards.

Wholesome treats. Years ago, Cheryl Thurston read an article about how teachers give conflicting messages. On one hand, they teach students about the importance of good nutrition. On the other hand, they give away candy as class rewards. Thurston thought the point was valid and, besides, she had been spending a lot of money on candy for prizes. The next day she announced, with mock-seriousness, that she could no longer in good conscience contribute to poor nutrition. From then on, she said, she would be giving only wholesome treats.

She began giving prizes of whatever wholesome food she happened to have in the house, the more ridiculous the better. The students would laugh (and groan) as she gave away a raisin, a piece of celery, a hunk of cheese, an unsalted Triscuit, a piece of tofu, a cauliflower flowerette or a bag of herbal tea. Much to her surprise, the students actually grew to prefer the wholesome treats, probably because they were so ridiculous.

Years later, Elaine Lundberg decided to use the idea in one of her workshops for teachers. She began by giving a potato as a prize, followed by a little packet of taco sauce from Taco Bell, a can of tuna, a brown banana, a turnip and a package of noodles. A week later, she ran into one of the teachers from the workshop in a local supermarket. He laughed about how much fun the wholesome treats had been, but went on to tell about sending one of his special education students off to a "mainstream" class

> **"Strange, when you come to think of it, that of all the countless folk who have lived before our time on this planet not one is known in history or in legend as having died of laughter."**
>
> **Max Beerbohm**
>
> (However, the *National Examiner* claimed otherwise on March 13, 1990, with these headlines: "Man laughs himself to death; clown accused of murder.")

for a period. When the student came back, the boy seemed baffled and angry.

"I won the game we played," he said, "but all I got was this *#@*****$% tartar sauce!"

Thus a warning: Not all classrooms are appropriate for wholesome treats. Many special education students won't under-  stand the joke. The approach might also be less successful with very young students. As always, use your head, and match the ideas to your personality and to the personality of the group.

Hall of fame. Another suggestion is a hall of fame for whatever form of excellence is appropriate in your class. It doesn't matter if your students are kindergartners, junior high school students or adults, if you have the right attitude. You might have a hall of fame for perfect test scores, for homework completed every day for a month, for those mastering the multiplication tables, for those who have written papers with no spelling errors, for those showing grace under pressure, for those coming up with a particularly creative solution to a problem — for whatever it is you would like to reward in your classroom.

You can add elegant touches, like lighting a candle, having the student wear a special hat or robe, playing dignified music like "Pomp and Circumstance" and presenting him or her with a certificate. Even if students complain good-naturedly and act as though you are crazy, they will get the message — that their good work is noticed and appreciated. Secretly, or not so secretly, they will be pleased.

Photographs. People love to see themselves in photographs. Try taking quick-developing snapshots of students or groups of students who deserve recognition. You might want to have some fun with the photograph sessions, having students wear special hats or hold special signs. You might even want to have props for the photos. For a science class, for example, you could have students stand behind a life-sized picture of Einstein, with the face cut-out.

You can then post the photos in your classroom, in a school display case, in the office or elsewhere. Students receive recognition, attention from others and — when you are finished with it — a photo to take home, perhaps with a quick note of congratulations.

Academy awards for class. If you videotape various student presentations during the school year, save the tapes for an end-of-the-year "Academy Awards for Class" ceremony. Go through the tapes and edit them, saving highlights to play back. You might give awards like "Best Performance in the Face of an Emergency," "Best Comedy Performance," "Best Supporting Actor," "Best Dramatic Performance" and "Best Imitation of a Famous Person."

Certificates. Design official-looking certificates on your computer, or get a supply of them at a business supply store. Be generous in awarding them throughout the year, perhaps at the end of each grading period, or any other time that you think students need special recognition. We know a five-year-old who graduated from kindergarten with "Honors in Imagination," and another who was named "Best Napper." A writing class of senior adults was thrilled to get certificates like "Most Skilled at Encouraging Others" and "Best at Capturing the Humor of Day-to-Day Life."

Teachers like to receive awards, too. However, we live in a world where those awards are few and far between. To make matters worse, we often miss opportunities to congratulate ourselves because we set up impossible standards. In our minds, many of us aspire to be Super Teachers, the teacher we think we should be — and know we are not. Super Teacher is . . . well, let's describe him or her in more detail . . .

★ Super Teacher

Super Teacher . . .

- always hands back papers the very next day
- never in her life has taken a sick day when she was not sick
- never in her life has taken a sick day when she *was* sick

Super Teacher . . .

- never forgets to draw circles around excused tardies on the attendance card
- reads all memos from the principal carefully, highlighting important parts with a yellow marker
- never pretends he didn't receive that important form that was supposed to be turned into the office yesterday at 3:00 PM

Super Teacher . . .

- never doodles during faculty meetings
- never dumps district communications into a folder labeled "junk"
- never forgets bus duty, not even accidentally

Super Teacher . . .

- appreciates the instant and frequent communication offered by the intercom system
- raises all window shades to the exact same height every afternoon before leaving school
- never complains if he doesn't have windows

Super Teacher . . .

- never thinks of dashing to 7-Eleven for milk on Saturday while she is wearing jeans, no bra and an old Grateful Dead T-shirt
- doesn't own an old Grateful Dead T-shirt
- doesn't know who the Grateful Dead are

Super Teacher . . .

- appreciates whatever the school board sees fit to pay
- welcomes the challenge of having 37 kids in a class
- schedules necessary surgery for spring break so she won't have to miss any school

(continued)

Super Teacher . . .

- doesn't sweat, not even in an un-airconditioned, 108° classroom
- never forgets to how to do double-sided copies on the Xerox machine
- never walks around with a streak of chalk dust on his behind

Super Teacher . . .

- has a great respect for fire drills, even when held at lunchtime during a blizzard
- never loses a child on the way to an assembly
- never has to go to the bathroom, except during her planning period

Super Teacher . . .

- never cringes when a child with the flu coughs on him
- never thinks of strangling students, not even for a moment, not even after 23 of them ask, separately, "What page is it on?"
- never yells

Super Teacher . . .

- never makes dire predictions about "how hard it's going to be when you get to junior high" (or to high school, or to college, or married)
- loves supervising school dances
- welcomes the challenge of being assigned remedial classes all day long

Super Teacher . . .

- loves the school spirit generated by "Grubby Day" or "Fifties Day" or "Dress Backwards Day"
- never creates a new bulletin board by just slapping up a free poster
- volunteers to be cheerleading sponsor every year

Super Teacher . . .

- loves being observed and evaluated by the principal, appreciating the valuable criticism offered
- never lectures students about "not thinking" or "setting an example" or "growing up"
- doesn't exist in real life

God doesn't write school textbooks

Some people act as though textbooks have a certain sacredness about them. They are wrong. God does not write school textbooks. (Perhaps she has too many other things to do!)

Sometimes we wonder who does. Recent studies have shown that many modern history texts, for example, are filled with factual errors. Other textbooks, so careful not to offend anyone or anything, are excruciatingly dull. Others are dated, and still others seem to be written by committees who have never actually encountered a real boy or girl.

If you are saddled with a terrible textbook, ancient equipment, a cold classroom or other problems, try this suggestion:

Turn weaknesses around through irreverence.

Sometimes the only thing you can do with a problem is to poke fun at it. Laughter can often turn minuses into pluses.

One teacher found herself having to lead a class through the boring grammar exercises in the back of the required textbook. As the students were yawning, a student read aloud a sentence about the creator of Birdseye frozen vegetables. The teacher lost her patience and started complaining about the authors of the textbook. "Of all the topics in the world to write sentences about, is this the best the authors could do? Did they think ninth graders would actually be interested in Birdseye frozen vegetables? Have they ever actually met a ninth grader?" The students laughed at her mini-tirade. Then they started paying attention, trying to be the first to note other sentences that were out of touch with a ninth grader's world. They called such sentences "Birdseye" sentences.

No, the students weren't paying as much attention to the grammar exercises as they were to finding stupid sentences, but at least they were paying some attention. At least there was a chance that they might actually pick up a smattering of grammar.

Poking fun at your textbook, if deserved, can help your students become critical

> **"A keen sense of humor helps us overlook the unbecoming, understand the unconventional, tolerate the unpleasant, overcome the unexpected, and outlast the unbearable."**
>
> **Dr. William A. Ward**

readers and critical thinkers. And poking fun at other problems can help everyone cope more effectively, even you.

If you are in a room without enough desks, insist that everyone be treated equally; have everyone sit on the floor one day. If your lectures are repeatedly interrupted by announcements over the intercom, have students try to predict the number of interruptions each day. If the district hand-outs have errors in them, offer prizes for those who can correct the most mistakes. Possibilities are endless, as are the problems most teachers have to work around in a typical school day.

Humor has so many uses in real life. In some circumstances, it can even be used to break bad news. Here's one example:

DEAR MOM,

I'VE ASKED THE RECEPTIONIST TO GIVE YOU THIS AS SOON AS YOU GET BACK FROM YOUR MEETING, SO YOU'LL KNOW WHERE I AM. MIKE'S MOM IS TAKING ME HOME WITH HER. SHE WAS THE ONLY PERSON AVAILABLE TO TAKE ME TO THE EMERGENCY ROOM. MY ARM ISN'T MOVING VERY WELL BECAUSE OF THE BANDAGES, SO I HOPE YOU CAN READ THIS OKAY.

THE FIREMEN SAID THE WIRING WAS VERY OLD. YOU'LL BE GLAD TO KNOW I SAVED THE FAMILY ALBUM. FLUFFY SHOULD BE OKAY, BUT IT DOESN'T LOOK SO GOOD FOR TIGGER.

ALSO, MY ALGEBRA TEACHER WANTS YOU TO GIVE HER A CALL.

LOVE,

Bobby

P.S. JUST KIDDING! I'M FINE, THE HOUSE IS FINE, AND FLUFFY AND TIGGER ARE FINE. I AM GETTING A "D-" IN ALGEBRA, THOUGH. WHAT A RELIEF, HUH? XXX

The girl with colitis goes by

Several years ago, the *Denver Post* ran an article on garbled song lyrics, with examples of lyrics that people had misinterpreted. One person thought "the girl with kaleidoscope eyes" from the Beatles' "Lucy in the Sky with Diamonds," was really *the girl with colitis goes by*. Another reader thought the 1985 song "One Night in Bangkok" was "I'm Not Ann Bancroft." Some thought the woman in the Kenny Rogers song "Lucille" was leaving the man with "four hundred children and a crop in the field," instead of with "four hungry children." One person thought the Beatles' "Paperback Writer" was "Pay for my Chrysler," and another thought Simon and Garfunkel were saying, "Are you going to start an affair?" instead of "Are you going to Scarborough Fair?"

We have all made such mistakes, which are often pretty funny. And we have all made more serious mistakes, which sometimes are not. Whenever appropriate, it helps to follow this advice:

Admit your mistakes and laugh at them.

When you laugh at yourself, you show students that mistakes are not the end of the world. Share past mistakes with your students. If you flunked chemistry three times, but final-

> **"The best thing about humor is that it shows people that they're not alone."**
>
> **Sid Caesar**

ly passed with a *B*, share that with struggling science students. Making light of your failure and concentrating on your eventual "triumph" can give students hope and help them feel they

are not alone. If you slip, trip, hiccup, or lose your train of thought, laugh at yourself. If you forget someone's name or misgrade a set of tests — admit your error and shake your head at your own fallibility.

It does take a certain confidence or flair to laugh at yourself. One teacher keeps a set of cue cards to use for her mistakes. When no one laughs at one of her jokes, for example, she holds up a "laugh" or "applaud" sign. She thus acknowledges that the material didn't go over and turns the failure itself into something for students to laugh about.

Wanted: Humor

You don't have to play the guitar to appreciate guitar music. You don't have to play football to enjoy football games. You don't have to be an artist to appreciate a wonderful drawing or painting. Similarly, you don't have to be funny yourself to appreciate humor and enjoy laughter. The next tip is one of the most important ones in this book:

Create an atmosphere where students know that humor is welcome.

Nothing will encourage humor more than simply appreciating it. In a welcoming atmosphere, humor thrives.

It is easy for a teacher to show that humor is welcome. When students are funny, reward them. Laugh. Praise. Share what they have done or said with others.

For example, if a student brings appropriate cartoons to class, post them. If someone composes a humorous response on a test, read it aloud. If someone writes a composition that is particularly funny, photocopy it to share with the class. Perhaps even consider adding a few bonus points in the grade book when someone is particularly clever or creative.

It is important to remember, however, that sometimes humor fails. A student will try too hard, overstep the bounds of good taste or make a "funny" remark that isn't funny. That doesn't mean you should stop encouraging

humor. Simply correct what is inappropriate and go on.

When you create an atmosphere where humor is clearly welcome and encouraged, everyone benefits. Humor enlivens the class, encourages students to tap their creativity and allows both you and your students to enjoy class more.

> **"Indicate the slightest willingness to laugh and jokes will walk right up to you, delivered by subordinates, peers, or even the boss. Look for it and expect it."**
>
> **Walter Kiechel**

An excerpt from
"The other funny thing in the classroom . . . kids"

If the environment has been established that allows the satirical remark, the ironic observation, the clever twist by a teenager, it will be forthcoming. Who would expect to find anything to laugh about in John Steinbeck's *The Pearl*? And yet I once had a sophomore who wrote an excellent paper of literary analysis with just that title: "Humor in the Pearl." His thesis was that the entire work was so unremittingly bleak and depressing that it could only be read as a satire of bleak, depressing literary construction. His paper was well written, his analysis thorough, and his wit bitingly clever.

Typical of a class that accepts expressions of humor in daily context was the student who came to take finals, bringing a stack of paper pirate hats from Long John Silver's restaurant. He placed the hats on the table next to the answer sheets for the final. Throughout the day, as class after class came to take finals, every student without comment picked up a pirate hat along with the answer sheet and wore it while taking the test. When an attendance clerk entered the room and appeared startled to see a room full of pirate-hatted students, they simply gazed at her, and one girl commented, "Thinking caps."

Perhaps a summative statement about the necessity of humor was made by Mark, a pleasant and agreeable senior. We had read Kafka's *Metamorphosis* and were comparing it to John Irving's *World According to Garp* and works by Kurt Vonnegut. I observed that some writers seem to express the idea that the only way to cope with "the undertoad" of life — the unseen and unexpected threat — is to look at it sideways, to find humor in the darkest situation, and not to take life or ourselves too seriously.

Mark looked very confused, his eyes wrinkled and his mouth half-open to speak, but hesitating. I asked what he was thinking: did he agree or disagree with this point of view? He responded, "But Mrs. Hickerson! What other way is there to look at life? It is funny! It has to be!"

Especially if your world is that of the classroom. I think Mark is right.

Benny Hickerson
English Journal, March 1989

A huge young man, dressed in black leather and chains, swaggered into my ninth-grade classroom one September. I groaned inside, jumping to conclusions about the kind of problem student I thought he would be.

I was wrong. Jeff was a gentle boy with a wry sense of humor, and he loved teasing me about cats. When we began studying poetry, Jeff took his teasing to new lengths. The following poem describes what happened:

Cheryl Thurston

★ Fluffy white kitty

His poems dealt with torture
and with death by bomb or axe.
He loved to make them gory, and
his emphasis was cats.

No matter what assignment
I would give to get him writing,
he wrote about a cat and always
ended with it dying.

He did it with a grin because
he loved to see me groan.
Because I fancied cats,
he wouldn't leave the things alone.

He wrote with wild abandon and
was endlessly quite clever.
But finally I said firmly,
"You can't torture cats forever.

"I want you to expand and
to attempt a new direction.
The subject for today, therefore,
is one of my selection —

"A white and fluffy kitty,
but you can't make this one cry.
You can't let this cat suffer,
and you can't let this cat die.

"With such a lovely topic,
I am confident and trusting
that this fluffy kitty poem
will have nothing that's disgusting."

He listened and he nodded;
then he worked until the bell.
"I've got the title now," he grinned—
"It's 'Fluffy White Kitty from Hell!'"

Reprinted from *Hide Your Ex-Lax Under the Wheaties* (Cottonwood Press, Inc.)

Were you adopted?

Elaine Lundberg has an older brother who is very gifted in math and who took a high school geometry class from a teacher named Mr. Bozza. When Elaine later showed up in Mr. Bozza's class, the teacher was delighted. Unfortunately, Elaine did not share her brother's talent. Math baffled her.

First she couldn't answer a simple question in class. Then she was unable to do a problem on the board. Finally, she flunked a test. Mr. Bozza looked at her sharply, but with a smile.

"Were you adopted?" he asked.

For Elaine, that was the right approach. They both laughed, mutually recognizing that she was not the math whiz her brother had been. The teacher then went on to give her the extra help she needed.

Sometimes a friendly kind of poking fun is effective in the classroom. With adults and children alike, the following tip can be very effective:

Tease — and be willing to be teased back.

Teasing can make people feel included, even special. It can motivate reluctant learners to become more involved. It can get across a serious point in a light-hearted way. It can add a friendly atmosphere to class. It can even show people that they are loved.

It is important to remember, however, that there are two kinds of teasing, kind and unkind. Obviously, teachers must use only teasing that is kind. Even then, we need to monitor students' reactions to our teasing. Students are not always accurate in their perceptions of how teasing is intended. At least one study has shown that they interpret teasing intended by the teaser as negative with 100% accuracy. However, they are only 65% accurate in correctly interpreting teasing that is intended by the teaser as positive. Students may not be as secure as we think they are, and it is a good idea to reassure them of our intentions when we tease, reminding them frequently that we wouldn't tease them unless we cared about them.

If we are going to tease, we have to be willing to be teased back. Though students love to tease, many teachers seem to have a fear of losing control if they allow teasing. That certainly does not need to happen. If students do occasionally step out of line — and occasionally they will — we need to remind them gently but

> **"Everybody likes a kidder, but nobody lends them money."**
> **Arthur Miller**

firmly that they have overstepped the bounds of good taste or respect, just as we do when they make mistakes in other areas. Why do we think that humor is an area where learning and making mistakes should be forbidden?

Can't you take a joke?

Some people use teasing as a weapon. A red warning flag should go up in your mind when you hear someone say, "What's the matter? Can't you take a joke?" That almost always refers to a remark that was not intended kindly. A few appropriate answers: "Yes, but I like kind humor, not cutting humor." Or "I certainly can. But my humor isn't the same as yours."

It's also perfectly fine to set limits on what we are willing to be teased about. One woman we know is perfectly willing to be teased about a number of things: her ability to get lost just about anywhere, her outspoken opinions, her uncanny ability to pick terrible men to date. However, she is not willing to be teased about her crooked teeth; they are a sensitive issue with her. Another answer to "Can't you take a joke?" is this one: "Sure I can. That's just not something I'm willing to joke about."

Sometimes, even with the best of intentions, our own teasing falls flat. If you see that someone perceives something you have said as negative, immediately apologize. You might say, "I'm sorry. That didn't come out right." Or "I'm sorry. I won't do that again."

Classic confusion

A number of years ago a junior high teacher had a cat named Ballou (as in the movie *Cat Ballou*). He also had a student who was quite a behavior problem and whose last name was Belew. One day the teacher was talking to a friend who had moved away. The friend, who had often heard the teacher complain about his student said, "How's Belew doing?"

"He died last month," said the teacher.

"Oh no!" said the friend. "How did he die?"

"Brain tumor. I was actually kind of relieved, in a way. He'd been behaving so strangely."

"Relieved? I mean, I know Belew was difficult, but isn't that a bit harsh?"

"No, he really was sick. At the end, he jumped into the bathtub with me and started walking on my stomach."

At that point the friend was quite convinced the teacher had lost his mind. It took awhile for them to unravel the confusion and see that the teacher was, of course, talking about the cat, while his friend was talking about the student.

A true story reprinted from
Mystery of the Suffocated Seventh Grader
(Cottonwood Press, Inc.)

When I taught junior high school, my students used to tease me about the instrument I play — the accordion. They gave me accordion cartoons and made accordion jokes and let me know in every way that playing the accordion is definitely not a "cool" thing to do.

Their teasing — and the teasing of my friends — eventually resulted in the founding of a national organization: Closet Accordion Players of America. Below are excerpts from the press release that resulted in newspaper articles, radio interviews and television stories all over the country:

Cheryl Thurston

Finally — it's safe to be an accordionist again.

Well, almost safe. The image of the accordionist still needs some sprucing up, but it is improving fast. Part of that is due to the efforts of Closet Accordion Players of America, a national organization dedicated to eliminating "accordion abuse" in America.

Four years ago, Colorado accordionist Cheri Thurston announced the formation of the group, and now there are over 1500 members from all over North America — including amateurs, professionals, classical accordionists, polka players, first-time players and people who just love accordion music. There are members who laugh about needing a "support group," and there are members who are deadly serious about their instrument. Closet Accordion Players of America accepts them all.

"It's easy to see the need for our group," said Thurston who has played the accordion since she was four years old. "People who admit to playing the accordion tend to look so sheepish about it, so ashamed. That's because of the way society portrays the accordion."

When television writers need to show that a character is a geek, they hand him an accordion. "Far Side" cartoonist Gary Larson has a cartoon that shows God saying, "Welcome to heaven . . . Here's your harp. Welcome to hell . . . Here's your accordion." Even television nerd Steve Urkel has taken up the accordion.

Thurston is a good sport. "You have to be if you play the accordion," she laughs. She laughs at accordion jokes and even pokes good-natured fun at the instrument herself, using humor to get attention for her cause. Despite the laughter, she really does think the accordion gets a bad rap.

Thurston has received hundreds and hundreds of letters from accordion lovers all over America who love her approach and her appreciation of the accordion. Recently CAPA sponsored an "Accordion Cool" contest to promote the image change needed for the instrument. The winner — a member who combines the incredibly hip sport of Rollerblading with accordion playing to get "Squeezeblading."

Thurston imagines the day when there will be groups all over America, meeting quietly in church basements and community centers. Each meeting will begin with one ordinary man or woman stepping to the microphone and saying, bravely, something like this:

"Hi, I'm Robert. I'm an accordion player."

And there will be people there who understand.

Some of us need to read body language better than English

It is amazing how many speakers have absolutely no sense of audience. Their listeners can be squirming, sitting with arms crossed, staring out the window, reading newspapers, even dozing off – and the speaker drones on and on, trying more of the same.

Good speakers have a sense of audience. So do good teachers. They pay attention to body language, and they know better than to keep plowing ahead

when they have lost a group's attention. They always keep this tip in mind:

When eyes start glazing over, do something different.

When everyone looks bored, everyone probably *is* bored. It's time to try something new. Often, laughter is a way to wake everyone up and lead a group back to the lesson at hand. What you do will depend upon your personality, the circumstances and the age and personality of your group.

Sometimes all that a class needs is a quick break. Have someone tell a joke. Have partners make funny faces at one another. Have younger students see how many times they can make a partner laugh in one minute.

You might even have an "emergency break" box that takes a bit of preparation ahead of time. A few ideas:

- Have a camera in the break box, as well as a pair of Groucho Marx glasses. Take a picture of a student wearing the glasses. The next time you need a break, take a snapshot of a different student wearing the glasses. Continue until you have a bulletin board full of shots of the whole class.

- Collect a wide variety of snapshots. (Students may want to contribute, too.) Pass out

the photographs, and have students write captions, using removable Post-it™ notes.

- Have a collection of funny songs ready to play at a moment's notice. Although we wouldn't use all of them with kids, here are some of our favorite funny songs: "I'm My Own Grandpaw," "I Don't Like Spiders and Snakes" and "Ahab The Arab" (Ray Stevens); "Jesus Loves Me But He Can't Stand You" (Austin Lounge Lizards); "Your Mind Is on Vacation, But Your Mouth Is Working Overtime" (Mose Allison); "Dentist" and "King

Tut" (Steve Martin); "Poisoning Pigeons In The Park" "Vatican Rag," and "Hunting Song" (Tom Lehrer); "Boy Named Sue" (Johnny Cash); and anything by Weird Al Yankovich.

- Have students make a quick list of funny-sounding words. A few examples: snort, hiccup, gulp, tickle, burp, wiggle, goofy, bump, zit.

"Laughter is the sensation of feeling good all over, and showing it principally in one spot."
Josh Billings

Whatever you try for a break, set a time limit, and keep it brief. Then get back to the subject at hand. Yes, you may have to teach students to get back on task quickly. If they have trouble settling down, point out that they are showing you they can't handle a break in routine. They will quickly learn to abide by the limits you set for breaks.

Besides a break, there are other techniques for regaining a group's attention. Here are a few ideas:

- Switch gears. If students have been listening have them *do* something – write, discuss, ask questions, draw pictures, perform experiments, whatever fits your subject. (See page 23, "Use activities, activities, activities!" for a discussion of how activities encourage laughter, as well as learning.)

- Ask questions. You can always call on students to wake them up, of course. Or, instead of asking a question yourself, call on a *student* to ask a relevant question of another student. If you make a habit of this, students are more likely to stay tuned in. The interchange between students can actually be more interesting, and sometimes more amusing, than traditional questions and answers between teacher and students.

- Switch roles. For a few minutes at a time, try having a student become the teacher,

reviewing a lesson with the class while you play the role of student. The change can be fun for both you and the group, and you will sometimes be surprised by the positive results.

Standing ovations

Silly as it may sound, students of all ages love standing ovations, especially when they occur in class. When someone does something that deserves a bit of recognition, say "That deserves a standing ovation!" Then have everyone stand and applaud. If the whole class manages to get back on time after lunch, announce a standing ovation for the whole group. If you get all your papers graded before the end of the day, ask for a standing ovation for yourself. Allow students themselves to ask for standing ovations – for anything they are proud of. Once in a while, have standing ovations for nothing special – Julie getting up to leave early for an orthodontist's appointment, for example, just to cheer her on. It's surprising how good it feels to get a standing ovation, even one that you've asked for yourself!

(We know one teacher who was very skeptical about standing ovations, until she finally decided to try them with one group. She was astonished at the positive atmosphere and good will that just two standing ovations helped create in one afternoon.)

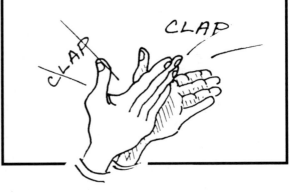

What are you, a comedian?

Elaine Lundberg does workshops on laughter and wellness, and she has performed as a stand-up comic in the Philadelphia area. When she attended her son's senior high Parents' Night a couple of years ago, she happened to make a funny remark as she arrived for one class. The other parents laughed, but the teacher did not. "What are you, a comedian?" he said. At that, even more parents started laughing, for they knew that she was. The teacher had probably used the line to squelch laughter in the past, but this time it didn't work.

Unfortunately, he is probably representative of teachers who try to fight laughter in their classrooms, who perhaps fear losing control. Here's a tip we think more teachers should follow:

When appropriate, encourage class comedians.

Teachers need not feel threatened by class comedians. Being funny in class is not a crime. In fact, being funny is a special gift that should be encouraged. Admittedly, class comedians sometimes overdo it, and they often need guidance in learning about limits, appropriateness and good taste. That's all right. Instead of being threatened by their antics, help them learn.

> **"I always wanted to be a stand-up comedian, but I was afraid people would laugh at me."**
> **Irv Furman**

Trying to squelch class clowns will only result in a power struggle that you are likely to lose. It is easier, and more fun, to get them on your side and to enjoy them as you help them learn proper boundaries.

A good sense of humor brings a lot of rewards in the real world. For one thing, people tend to gravitate to those who laugh easily and who make others laugh. A sense of humor is also an asset in the work place, especially in positions with a lot of stress. One study has found that corporations consider the lack of a sense of humor a serious handicap when hiring executives.

Another study shows that adult groups that contain a "wit" tend to perform better than other groups, being more task-oriented and showing higher morale and greater success at problem-solving. Isn't it possible that class clowns in school may have the same effect on their groups?

When you become annoyed at your own class clowns, stop and consider for a moment the teachers who had the following individuals in class:

* Jay Leno
* Jim Carrey
* Billy Crystal
* Joan Rivers

- Jerry Seinfeld
- Bette Midler
- Bill Cosby
- Carol Burnett
- Eddie Murphy
- Ellen DeGeneres
- Dennis Miller
- Mike Myers
- Al Franken
- Whoopie Goldberg

It's very possible that these comedians got their very first laughs in the classroom!

In eighteenth-century Berlin, philosopher Moses Mendelssohn is said to have collided with a Prussian officer while walking down the street. The officer yelled, "Swine!" Mendelssohn just tipped his hat, bowed and replied, "Mendelssohn."

Class clowns I have known and loved

Some of my fondest classroom memories involve class clowns. Years ago, I had a seventh grader named Jim Brewer who was one of the funniest people I have ever known. He could do a pantomime, on the spot, on any given topic, and everyone would be in stitches. Something about him was so funny that I could hardly talk to him without laughing.

I wound up using Jim to help my students get their work done and stay on task. I would simply announce sometimes that if everyone cooperated, I would save the last three minutes of class for Jim to perform on a topic of their choice. It worked like a charm. The kids always got right to work, and Jim had an appreciative audience for his talents. The last I heard, Jim had grown up and become a disc jockey in Alaska. I often imagine how his humor must be a real asset in his job.

Years later, another student named Hunter Schoemacher kept me laughing all year long. Hunter hated cats, or at least he pretended that he did after he discovered that I loved them. From then on, every single paper he turned in that year had on it, somewhere, a picture of a cat drawn in the crosshairs of a gun. Each varied slightly, but they all looked something like this:

His pictures never failed to make me laugh as I came across them unexpectedly in a pile of papers. He also used the joke in other ways, as well. Once, when we were studying quotation marks, I gave the students a block of unpunctuated dialogue, which they were to rewrite and punctuate correctly. Though the text was about a boy asking a girl out for a date, Hunter's test was turned in as a dialogue between a cat hater and his teacher. It was cleverly written — even to the point of being sure to include every skill I was testing the students on. Of course, his test had to be shared with the class, providing laughter as well as more reinforcement on the proper use of quotation marks. I was always glad that Hunter knew me well enough to know that his cleverness would be not only accepted but appreciated.

Cheryl Thurston

Excess, excess, excess

If lectures worked terribly well, parents wouldn't have kids who leave their dirty socks in the middle of the floor. Teachers wouldn't have students who refuse to do their homework. Employers wouldn't have workers who always show up late.

Unfortunately, serious lectures don't usually change behavior. Mock-serious lectures are often

more successful. If you are a person with a flair for exaggeration, try the following tip:

Beat a subject to death, to the point of absurdity.

Sometimes it pays to overdo, if you can do it with a sense of humor. Remind students of an important point — again and again and again. Take every opportunity, no matter how small, to lecture them about one of your pet peeves. Let anything and everything remind you of a lesson you want them to learn.

> **"Against the assault of laughter nothing can stand."**
>
> **Mark Twain**

If you really beat a subject to death, your lectures can become funny and instructive as well. Before long, students will get your message, even as they laugh at the ridiculous measures you take to get it across.

Cheryl Thurston has found that overdoing can sometimes be quite successful in the English classroom. She carries on and on about some of her pet peeves, like spelling "a lot" as one word or throwing commas into a sentence for no good reason. At the end of school one year, a ninth grade boy wrote her the note below, which illustrates all of her pet peeves, and then some. Clearly, the boy had been listening!

Ms. thurstin:
this has been one of my favorite english classes, i learned more this year than in any english class up to this point? the, comma, section was ve,ry helpful. I wish we could hav spended more time on speeking, though,.! Thanks alot, your a Great teacher.

Gavin Whitrock

How is a fraction like a toasted cheese sandwich?

What kind of questions do teachers usually ask? Questions to which we know the answers — or, more often, *the* answer. We usually know the direction we want a class to go, and we work hard to point it in that direction. Sometimes, however, it can be exciting, fascinating, and humorous to let go of control and try the following idea:

Ask students to compare unrelated items.

When students compare seemingly unrelated items, they are really forced to think. An especially effective approach is to ask students a comparison question to which you admit you don't have an answer. When there is no right answer, the students feel challenged to use their creative powers. The results may surprise you.

> **"Wit consists in seeing the resemblance between things which differ and the difference between things which are alike."**
> **Madame de Stael**

One teacher decided to test this idea by asking her students a question to which she couldn't think of a single possible answer: "How is a jar of peanut butter like a train?" In just a few moments, a student raised her hand and said, "They both have a 'choo' (chew)." The teacher decided to ask more questions that she couldn't answer, and she was almost always surprised at how inventive her students could be when they were not searching for one right answer.

Comparisons are an excellent way to review material the class has been studying or has studied in the past. For example, a reading class might answer this questions: "How is *Charlotte's Web* like *A Wrinkle in Time*?" Here are a few more examples, from a number of subject areas:

Geography

How is the Sahara Desert like the North Pole?

Home economics

How is breakfast like a calorie?

Biology

How is the human heart like photosynthesis?

History

How was the Revolutionary War like the War in the Persian Gulf?

Astronomy

How is the Milky Way like the moon?

English

How is a sonnet like a research paper?

Another approach — sometimes more fun — is to ask students to compare something you have been studying to something outside the classroom. Here are just a few examples from different subject areas:

Math

How is a fraction like a toasted cheese sandwich?

English

How is Lady Macbeth in *Macbeth* like Cher in *Clueless*?

Science

How is an amphibian like MTV?

Music

How is folk music like hip-hop?

Home Economics

How is the basic food pyramid like a football game?

Geography

How is a tropical rain forest like a school bus?

Art

How was the artist Michelangelo like a video game?

Droodles

Completing droodles is a good way to stretch the mind muscle. There are no right or wrong answers. The objective is to open the mind to creative possibilities in identifying each picture. Here is one example:

What is this?

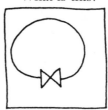

(One possibility: a butterfly skipping rope)

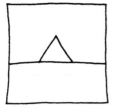

(A shark in the bathtub)

(A bubble gum blowing champion)

(A man falling off a tightrope)

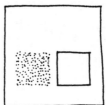

(Unassembled sandpaper)

Thou Dost Offend Me!

When attending a Renaissance fair, where characters roamed the park dressed as kings, knights and ladies, Elaine Lundberg approached a costumed gentleman and asked where she might find a restroom. The knight, remaining in character, looked at her in shock and said, "Prithee, madame, thou dost offend me!"

If you are a born actor — and many teachers are — have some fun with this tip:

Be someone else.

Many teachers can create memorable lessons by pretending to be someone else. A history teacher might show up one day dressed as Abraham Lincoln, and acting the part. An English teacher might appear as Edgar Allan Poe or Emily Dickinson, a science teacher as Charles Darwin, an art teacher as Vincent Van Gogh, a music teacher as Beethoven. Such a performance takes some research and preparation the first time through, but the students are likely to remember the visit well. Yes, there will be laughter and disbelief at first, but for teachers with a bit of "ham" in them, a special appearance can be extremely effective.

Instead of portraying a specific individual from history, another approach is to portray a person from a certain era. One history teacher we know has a wardrobe for every unit he teaches. He comes to school as a cave man, a Medieval peasant, a Roman statesman, a Civil War soldier, etc. as the school year progresses. Students are allowed to question him about life in his time period, and they learn a great deal from his presentations.

> **"Good teaching is one-fourth preparation and three-fourths theatre."**
>
> **Gail Godwin**

Another idea is to let a student "be" a famous person for a class period, giving a talk and answering questions from the class. In order to give an accurate presentation, the student will need to do a lot of research and preparation, perhaps as a special project or for extra credit.

The world will not end because Heather has gum in class, again

It is so easy to become absorbed in rules, report cards, homework, track meets, etc. — narrowing our view of the world to the confines of the school grounds. Sometimes we lose perspective. The world won't end if Heather has gum in class again, or if Jason is drawing Godzilla-like creatures on his math homework. Sometimes, the best way to brighten our days is to try the following:

Lighten up.

We don't always need to take everything so seriously. Teaching isn't—and shouldn't be— a deadly-serious job. Sometimes reacting with a sense of humor can save a situation.

> **"They that are serious in ridiculous things will be ridiculous in serious affairs."**
>
> **Cato the Elder**

An excellent teacher we know has won awards for her teaching, including being named a state teacher of the year. One day, years ago, she walked into her ninth grade classroom after lunch and began a lesson. The kids started giggling, so she stopped, looked at the group and said, "Come on now. What's going on?"

They pointed to the board.

She looked. There, drawn in great detail across the front of the room, was an enormous penis. The kids went into hysterics.

Now what would most of us have done? We might have gone into our "inappropriate for class" routine, talking about immaturity and good taste. Or we might have become angry, tried to find the culprit, and tried to punish him or her. We might have shaken our head at such immaturity and simply erased the board, voicing our disappointment—only to find another body part drawn on the board the next day, and another part the next day.

This woman, however, had real presence of mind. Quickly, she saw the ridiculousness of her predicament and ran through possibilities in her mind. In the end, she simply looked at the drawing for a moment, turned to the class and said, "Well, my goodness. It's a penis. And such a well-drawn penis! Look at the detail. Why, I just can't believe someone in this class could draw such a penis. Such artistry!" She went on and on, using the word "penis" dozens of times, and not showing a bit of anger or disapproval. It soon became clear who had made the drawing, for the boy turned a darker and darker shade of red as he sank slowly in his seat, mortified, even though the teacher never acknowledged him in any way.

Everyone laughed. Self-conscious teenagers squirmed and giggled at her unabashed use of the word "penis." When the teacher finished her extravagant praise of the drawing, she simply erased it and continued her lesson.

There wasn't one word of reprimand. Better yet, no one in that class ever drew on her blackboard again.

Sometimes we forget that kids are kids. We tell them that they are acting immature, and of course they are. That is because they *are* immature. They are supposed to be. We often expect them to act like adults when they are not adults.

As teachers, we need to keep some perspective. We also need to be careful not to become threatened too easily. The world will not end if we laugh at the absurdity of things, and there are certainly plenty of absurdities to laugh at in the world of teaching.

During the Nazi regime, a joke could be considered an act against the Fuehrer or against the Nazi state. Hitler even had special "joke courts" which could punish people for such offenses as naming their dog or horse Adolph. Making the government look wrong or funny was no laughing matter in the Third Reich.

A man called home to check up on things while he was away on vacation. His younger brother answered the phone and said everything was all right, except that his cat was dead. The older brother was appalled at his lack of sensitivity and told him he should have broken the news to him more gently. "First you could have said, 'Your cat's up on the roof and won't come down,'" he explained. "Then, the next time I called, you could have said, 'Your cat fell off the roof and is pretty badly hurt.' Then the next time, you could have told me that my cat died."

The next day the older brother called again. "How is everything?" he asked.

"Oh, all right, except that Mom's up on the roof and won't come down."

Stop in the Name of Love

When giving a spelling test to her special education students, Elaine Lundberg always tried to make the exam entertaining. Her favorite spelling word was "stop." Whenever she read that word, she would proceed to sing and dance "Stop, in the Name of Love" by the Supremes. Her middle school students looked at her quizzically but laughed.

One day two of her boys ran into the room, all excited because they had heard "her song" on MTV! After that, she always threw in the word "stop" on spelling tests for extra credit, and the whole class would burst into song.

Some weeks later, when Lundberg had recess duty, a youngster started to chase a ball across a busy street. "STOP!" she yelled at the top of her lungs.

Twelve developmentally disabled youths immediately sang out, "in the name of love!"

Sometimes we all worry too much about how we might appear if we were to sing, dance, show emotion or take some other kind of risk. As a consequence, we miss a lot of opportunities. It can be helpful to any teacher to remember the following tip:

Don't be afraid to look foolish once in awhile.

Teachers shouldn't be afraid to look foolish once in a while. Sometimes students learn the most when we plunge right into a lesson and do something memorable, something silly, something outrageous, something that really makes our students remember, think, feel or care.

> **"Most folks are about as happy as they make up their minds to be."**
>
> **Abraham Lincoln**

Sing, dress up in a costume, accept a dare, recite a poem, enter a contest, share a personal moment — (without worrying about how you will look.) It's a risk that can very well pay off.

For example, for the past few years many principals have started challenging their students by promising to complete a certain "dare" if students meet a goal. One Pennsylvania elementary school principal demonstrated his willingness to look foolish. In the spring of 1992, Bruce Burt challenged his first through fifth grade students to read at least 3600 books over the summer. If they did, he promised that he would shave off his beard for the first time since 1976 — and in public.

The students came through, reading a total of 3639 books, or an average of more than six per student. Burt's barber came to school that fall. In front of the school's 568 students, he shaved off the principal's beard. Burt probably didn't look terribly dignified in the barber's chair, but his students gained from his willingness to take a risk.

Tee-hee

In her therapy sessions, California therapist Annette Goodheart, Ph.D., has her patients say "tee-hee" after telling about a problem, even a very serious problem. Somehow, the words "tee-hee" help make the problem less important. The problem starts to lose its power over the individual. You might try the same technique with your own problems, large and small. Or you might help your students learn to put problems into perspective with the technique. Try statements like these, or have your students try them:

"The copy machine hates me . . . tee-hee!"

"I can't possibly get all these papers graded by tomorrow . . . tee-hee!"

"Bobby pushed my notebook off my desk! . . . tee-hee!"

"The hard drive on my computer just crashed . . . tee-hee!"

It's hard to stay stressed or angry when a "tee-hee" comes out of your mouth.

The helping verb cheer

One of my strongest memories of seventh grade is of Mrs. Wall doing the helping verb cheer. I remember her as about 55 years old (although to my 12-year-old eyes, anyone over 21 probably looked 55), gray-haired and tall. She had put all of the helping verbs into a chant-like "cheer," and she would stand at the front of the room, making us repeat the cheer after her. She would throw her arms out like a cheerleader, shout and show great enthusiasm for those 33 little words, which I can still recite:

Is! Be! Am! Are! Was! Were! Been!
Has, have, had!
Do, does, did!
Can, could!
Shall, should!
Will, would!
May, might (and) must!

There isn't anything much duller than learning the helping verbs, but Mrs. Wall made it exciting. Sure, she probably looked a bit foolish up there cheering, but it worked.

Mrs. Wall wasn't afraid to look foolish about more serious subjects, either. She loved the poem "Gunga Din," by Rudyard Kipling, and she let us know it. She talked about that poem with great enthusiasm, and she read it with emotion. When she played a recording of it for the class, her eyes filled with tears. Because I had never seen anyone show such emotion about a work of literature, I paid attention. What could make an adult carry on so? I wondered. I listened, and I understood.

Showing our serious side to students can be as much of a risk as showing our silly side — but it's often a risk worth taking.

Cheryl Thurston

A strange sort of science

When I was in school, nothing terrified me more than complicated scientific formulas, microscopes that revealed strange life forms and dead animals floating in formaldehyde. To me, science seemed rigid, dry and just plain boring.

But when I was 15, Mr. Smiley and Mr. Natalie came along. Mr. Smiley did experiments on clay figures that he named Mr. Bill, after the figure on "Saturday Night Live." Mr. Smiley would crush, pressurize, blow up and flambé his little Mr. Bills, and it was hard not to laugh at a grown man yelling, "Oh noooooooooooo, Mr. Bill!" Afterwards, he would show us what was left of Mr. Bill and warn: "Now this is what could happen to you, if you don't understand the chemical changes that affect the composition, structure and properties of substances. Don't be another Mr. Bill!" We would listen and learn.

In his science class, Mr. Natalie had a lab that everyone dreaded, for we had to dissect a bull's eye. On the day we were to begin dissecting, Mr. Natalie showed up in a T-shirt with a giant eye on the front of it, and he was carrying a portable stereo. "I decided to be as truly tasteless as I could be about this experiment," he said. "Therefore, I have here a collection of songs just right for the occasion — songs about eyes. Yes, an entire hour of songs about eyes!"

In spite of myself, I was laughing as I began to slice and pull apart the eye, examining the retina, cornea, iris and lens. Meanwhile, Mr. Natalie ran around the room, and when he wasn't helping students, he was hamming it up. He jumped around tables, holding a bull's eye in front of his face and singing along as he played songs like "Eye In the Sky" (The Alan Parsons Project), "Eye of the Tiger" (Survivor), "For Your Eyes Only" (Sheena Easton), "Don't It Make My Brown Eyes Blue" (Crystal Gayle) and the grand finale, "She Blinded Me With Science" (Thomas Dolby).

Looking back, I see that Mr. Natalie and Mr. Smiley were able to grab our attention, make us think and make potentially disgusting or difficult experiments interesting and fun — all by using humor. For the first time, I wasn't afraid or intimidated. By laughing at the very things that scared me, I was able to get over my fears, sit back and learn.

Rory Franklin

Do we get to do anything fun today?

One English teacher we know got tired of his eighth graders coming into the room asking, "Do we get to do anything fun today?" He started giving them a different answer each day: "Yes, I thought today we would put a net up over the desks and play volleyball." Or "Yes, I've decided to take you all to an amusement park today to ride the roller coaster." Or "Yes, I thought today we would sample pizza to decide who makes the best kind in town." His outrageous answers soon became in themselves a source of fun in his classroom. Although "fun" certainly isn't the goal of education, there are many activities for the classroom that are educational and fun to do. Most teachers enliven their classrooms, from time to time, with the following idea:

Play a game.

Students generally enjoy games in the classroom, and they learn from them as well. Often, they are especially useful for reviewing less-than-exciting material. A few games that are fun for students and effective as well:

Review Baseball. To help students review information before a test, set up a baseball diamond in your room, with three bases and a home plate. (Construction paper taped to the floor works just fine.) Divide the class into two teams, and as each player comes "to bat," ask if he or she wants a one-base, two-base, three-base or home-run question. (Naturally, home-run questions are more difficult than one-base questions.) If a student answers correctly, he or she advances to the correct base. If someone is already on that base, that student is "bumped" ahead one base. If a student misses a question, the miss is an "out" for that team. Three "outs," and the other team comes to bat.

Classroom Trivial Pursuit. You can play your own version of the popular Trivial Pursuit ™ board game, using questions from your subject area as questions. Or use the cards from the real game as a "filler" for the last few minutes of class.

> **"Humor is your own smile surprising you in the mirror."**
> **Langston Hughes**

Hot Potato. Toss a Nerf ™ ball or other light ball to a student. Ask a review question to that student. If he or she answers correctly, have the student throw the ball to someone else, and ask a new question. If the student misses, he or she throws to someone else, who attempts to answer the same question. The game can also be played in teams, with the ball going to the opposite team whenever anyone misses.

Desperate Games for Desperate Times. Sometimes there are desperate days at school — in particular, the last few days of school. You've got special assemblies and book check-in and hot afternoons with no air conditioning. You've got kids whose minds seem to have checked out days ago, but whose bodies are still in your classroom bouncing off the walls — or so it seems.

For times like these, most of us have a few games to rely on when we are desperate. No, they aren't games our professors in graduate school would approve of, for they don't have much educational value. Actually, they may have no educational value, unless you look at "keeping the lid on," "helping them avoid killing one another" and "maintaining teacher sanity" as educational value. Many of us do.

Desperate times call for desperate measures. Consider adding the following games to your emergency bag of tricks. They have absolutely nothing to do with any school subject, but at least some of them do encourage creativity. More important, they are relatively quiet games that will keep students interested, and usually smiling, at a hectic time of year.

Here Comes the Judge.
Have one student put a "scribble" on the board, repeating it four times in different places. The student then leaves the room, and four students come forward to fill in the scribbles, making them look like something identifiable, and in one minute. Then the original student comes back into the room and judges the results, determining which drawing he or she thinks is the most original and creative completion of the scribble. Here is an example of a scribble and the way four students completed it:

 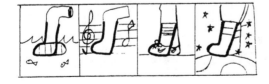

Silent Ball.
If you have flat-topped desks, have students sit on top of them. Toss a Nerf ™ ball into the group, and let students toss the ball to one another, without getting off their desks. When a student misses the ball, he or she must sit down in the desk seat, unless the person throwing threw the ball out of reach. (In that case the person throwing the ball must sit down.) The tossing must be done in silence, so any person who speaks must also take his or her seat. The person who remains on the desk top longest is the winner.

If you don't have flat-topped desks, students can stand beside their desks and sit down in their seats when they miss the ball. It's a good idea to designate a referee to settle disputes that arise (usually about whether or not a missed ball was thrown out of reach.)

Silent Pictionary.
Most of your students are probably familiar with Pictionary™, a board game that can be purchased in stores all over the country. While the standard game can be played in a classroom, using the chalkboard instead of paper, it is difficult if you have more than ten or fifteen students. When twenty-five or thirty students are shouting guesses, it is almost impossible for the game to progress, just because of the noise level. Instead, you might try playing Silent Pictionary with your students. First divide the class into two teams. Have the students move their desks so that everyone is sitting in pairs, a Team #1 member beside a Team #2 member. For ease in scoring points later, be sure that all Team #1 members sit on the same side of each pair of students, so that you can easily recognize the teams.

Explain that Silent Pictionary is played much the same as regular Pictionary™, except that all responses are written rather than spoken or shouted. The object of the game is for one team to accumulate more points than the other team. Students win points by guessing words correctly, but they lose points by talking or shouting out answers while the illustrators draw.

To begin, toss a coin to see which team illustrates first. Ask several "illustrators" to come forward. (The number of illustrators depends upon the amount of chalkboard space you have; three students usually works well.)

Pick a card from a purchased Pictionary ™ game. Show the illustrators the card and the selection that they are to draw, following regular Pictionary™ rules. Then give them all one minute to illustrate. (All the illustrators draw the same item at the same time.) As the illustrators draw, class members write down their guesses.

At the end of one minute, see how many people have guessed correctly. (Having opposing team members seated next to one another has one objective: to keep everybody honest.) Record the number of correct guesses for each team. Then have three more illustrators come forward and select the next item from a Pictionary™ card.

Guessing in silence is a challenge, particularly for young people. If anyone talks or shouts out an answer, deduct one point for that team. (Yes, teams can go into negative numbers.) Try to keep the game moving as quickly as possible, but do allow a few moments after each round for students to laugh or comment on the illustrations and guesses.

Eraser Chase. Three students come to the front of the class. Designate one "chaser" and two "chasees." Then place a chalkboard eraser on each student's head. The chaser then tries to catch and tag one of the chasees — but without allowing the eraser to fall from his or her head. Similarly, the chasees try not to let their erasers fall. Whenever an eraser falls, that person is

replaced by another student in class. If one of the chasees is caught, he or she is replaced as well.

Also, all chasers and chasees must keep moving at all times; no one is allowed to stand quietly in the corner to keep the eraser from falling off.

"**M**ommy, mommy!" cried the little boy. "My turtle is dead!"

Concerned about her son's first brush with death, the mother put her arm around him and said, "That is very sad. We will wrap him in tissue paper, put him in a shoe box and have a burial ceremony in the backyard. Afterwards, we'll go out for ice cream and then buy you a new pet. I don't want you to . . ." She stopped suddenly, for she saw the turtle move. "Johnny, your turtle moved! It's not dead after all!"

"Oh," said the disappointed boy. "Can I kill it?"

YOU KNOW IT'S GOING TO BE A BAD DAY WHEN YOU FIND THE "SIXTY MINUTES" TELEVISION CREW WAITING OUTSIDE YOUR HOMEROOM.

Toothpick bridges and two-story egg drops

All too often in schools, it is the gifted classes where something really interesting is going on. We've all heard about contests where students try to build a toothpick bridge that will support many pounds of weight or where students try to construct containers that will allow an egg to survive a drop off a three-story building. Such challenging activities shouldn't be limited to

the gifted classroom. Even the most apathetic students are often motivated when you challenge their creativity. Give the following idea a try:

Encourage creativity by assigning an outrageous task.

Creativity and humor are kissing cousins. Encouraging creativity will encourage humor, as well as thinking. Often, creativity stirs most when the challenge is a fairly ridiculous one.

Suppose, for example, that you want students to learn a process, rather than just a set of facts. Try inventing a ridiculous task that will help them learn the serious process.

> **"Comedy is the last refuge of the nonconformist mind."**
> **Gilbert Selds**

For example, we once heard about an English teacher who was teaching students how to write a research paper — including how to use note cards, write footnotes, compile a bibliography, write a thesis statement, prove a thesis, etc. Instead of assigning a typical subject for research, the teacher had the students "prove" anything at all that they wanted in their papers, so long as it was absolutely ridiculous. (Exam-

ples: Since 1960, the Republican party has been controlled by alien beings. Music video is the most important educational tool of the twentieth century. Environmental pollution is a myth. Computer technology is just a passing fad. Congress should pass legislation requiring every American family to have at least one goldfish.)

The students were required to go through all the steps of writing a research paper, except that they didn't have to do the actual research. They simply made up their "facts," supporting their thesis statements with nonexistent research, false studies and phony quotations. The students still had to learn about supporting a thesis, and they still had to learn all the mechanics involved in producing a finished paper. However, doing actual research was put off until a later assignment, so that students did not have to learn everything at once. The outrageous topic allowed them some fun as they learned the basics, and it was easier for students to make the transition then to actually researching a topic for a serious paper.

The outrageous tasks you can invent for your students are limited only by your imagination. Here are just a few ideas to get you to thinking:

English

Being careful to support your thesis, write a persuasive paper proving that the next President of the United States should be someone under twelve years of age.

Home economics

Create a piece of wearable clothing, using a black garbage bag.

Math

Write and solve a story problem about traveling to Philadelphia in a '71 Volkswagen.

Geography

Write a rap song about teenagers and the tundra.

Science

As the result of a vote by extremists, the law of gravity is to be eliminated in your city next month. As mayor of that city, outline the problems and the solutions you have in store for the area.

Art

Design and draw a more functional human face for the future.

Physical education

Create a new kind of solitaire game for busy professional men and women who have little time to exercise. Make the game one that can be played alone in fifteen minutes or less, but that will provide aerobic exercise and tone muscles.

Music

Write and perform a song about nail clippers or mayonnaise—or nail clippers *and* mayonnaise.

Bad jokes

Sometimes bad jokes are as much fun as good ones. To fill a few odd minutes at the end of class, try a bad joke-a-thon and see how many "groaners" your group can tell. Here are a few to get them started:

What's brown and wrinkled and lives in a church tower? The Lunch Bag of Notre Dame.

Little Jason came up to his teacher and asked, "Would you ever be mad at me for something I didn't do?"

"Why, of course not, Jason. I would never be mad at you for something you didn't do."

"That's good," smiled Jason. "I didn't do my homework."

Hilary's teacher frowned at her as she slipped into class. "You are late again," the teacher said. "Doesn't your watch tell you what time it is?"

"No," answered Hilary. "I have to read it."

What's green, has twenty-two legs and plays football? The Green Bay Pickles.

What was wrong with the restaurant they opened on the moon? It lacked atmosphere.

What's purple and goes "slam, slam, slam, slam?" A four-door grape.

What do you get when a piano falls down a mine shaft? A-flat minor.

What's worse than biting into an apple and finding a worm? Finding half a worm.

What's black and white and green and black and white? Two zebras fighting over a pickle.

How do you catch a unique rabbit? Unique up on them. How do you catch a tame rabbit? The tame way.

Why can't *A Fish Called Wanda* ever win?

Just once we wish a movie like *A Fish Called Wanda* could win an Academy Award. Once in a while a comedy is nominated, but does it ever win? No. It is because of humor discrimination. People refuse to take humor seriously. Because they laugh at it, they unconsciously assume that it must be easy to write, easy to perform. They assume it must be somehow "less" than a movie on a serious subject.

People who have written, directed or performed comedy know better. It takes every bit as much skill, and perhaps more, to successfully pull off something funny. Part of that is because people laugh at very different things. They become teary-eyed at similar subjects — death, abandoned children, injured puppies, for example. But what they find humorous is, well, just about anything — including death, abandoned children and injured puppies, at least in some circumstances.

Humor itself is a fascinating topic. When you are planning lessons, don't forget this idea:

Use humor as an area for classroom exploration

If you have career day, invite a comedian, a clown, a humor writer or a cartoonist to your classroom. A career in humor isn't any less legitimate than any other career, just because laughter is involved.

If your students are doing research, encourage them to research topics like the history of animation, the development of a cartoonist like Walt Disney or Gary Larson, the career of a comedian like Roseanne or Jerry Seinfeld, or the life of a humorist like Mark Twain. If they are writing in classroom journals, ask them to write about "a time you made

someone laugh" or "a time someone made you laugh" or "something you think is really funny." Ask them to try to explain what makes something funny to them.

> **"Comedy is acting out optimism."**
> **Robin Williams**

If students are learning to compare and contrast, consider having them compare and contrast two humorous stories, movies, jokes or cartoon strips. If they are learning interview techniques, have them interview a funny radio disc jockey or someone from an advertising agency who does humorous television commercials or radio spots. If you just want to get them thinking and exploring ideas, have them analyze a television character they enjoy, trying to figure

57

out just what it is that makes the character funny.

If you are open to opportunities for integrating humor as a subject into your curriculum, you will be surprised at how often you can enrich your classroom in unusual and effective ways.

Before the collapse of Communism, two Soviets, Natasha and Rudolph, were sitting down to dinner. "It looks like snow," remarked Natasha.

"Nyet," answered Rudolph. "It looks like rain."

Sure enough, it soon started to rain. Rudolph looked at Natasha with an I-told-you-so expression on his face. "Rudolph the Red knows rain, dear," he said proudly.

Teacher trivia

Committee, staff and department meetings are often a necessary nuisance in education. To wake up group members and make them slightly happier to be in attendance, take turns conducting trivia contests as people arrive for a meeting. Make the trivia questions about staff members and your school. Sample kinds of questions: What teacher on our staff once rode a llama in the Andes? What memorable gift did Mr. Honer receive from a student in 1988? When did this school start serving hot lunches? Which teacher attended prom with a future Senator from our state?

Mind pictures

Teach students the value of creating absurd mind pictures in order to remember lists. At the same time you will be teaching sequencing, association and memory skills.

For example, suppose that you need to go to the store to get a can of tuna, some bandages, a sack of oranges, milk and a pair of panty hose — and you can't find a pencil and paper. Create a ridiculous image in your mind, relating the items. Perhaps you would imagine bandages plastered all over a can of tuna, which is balancing on top of the oranges. At the same time, wearing a pair of panty hose over your head, you would be pouring milk over the whole thing. The ridiculous image will help you remember your list.

Good morning, honorable teacher

One teacher we know is a karate expert who also works with students with behavior problems. He borrows from the martial arts for his classroom. Every day, as his students enter the room, they must give a bow of respect, with the greeting, "Good morning, honorable teacher." It's all done with a sense of humor, yet the tone for class is

set by this morning ritual. For these students, the exaggerated show of respect helps them see how they really are supposed to act. Sometimes kids only "get" something when we overdo it. In many situations, the following idea is very helpful:

Use exaggeration for humor — and effect.

Exaggeration has all kinds of uses in the classroom. Suppose, for example, that your students can't seem to speak one sentence without using the word "like" seven or eight times. ("Like, I was really, like, into this guy, and he, like, you know, dumped me for this, like, totally

> **"Only by attempting the absurd, can we achieve the impossible."**
>
> **Anonymous**

boring girl with, like, no personality.") Insist one day that everyone use the word "like" as much as possible. Set the tone by using it to an exaggerated degree in everything you say, and then keep it up, even when it is starting to drive everyone crazy. The exaggeration will help students become aware of how much they use the word in their own speech — and awareness is the first step in learning to break a habit.

Other uses:

- Give exaggerated demonstrations of how *not* to do something. Examples: How *not* to organize a notebook, how *not* to give a speech, how *not* to take notes during a lecture.

- Have exaggerated demonstrations of the absolutely perfect way to do something. Suppose, for example, that you want students to be more polite to one another during class discussions. You might have two students model a class discussion, carrying politeness to ridiculous extremes. The conversation might go something like this:

Student #1: Excuse me, Holly. But when you have finished with your point, perhaps you will allow me to add something. I don't want to rush you, but I am eager to react to what you are saying.

Student #2: Why, of course, Timothy. I see that I have dominated the conversation, and

I do apologize. It was thoughtless of me not to give you a chance. I know that whatever you have to say will add a lot.

Students will laugh, but they will get the point, as well.

- Have students come up with answers to "what if" questions. The process provides a valuable exercise in thinking and using the imagination. For example, you might ask students, "What if no one in this country learned to add decimals anymore?" They might come up with something like this:

Young people wouldn't be able to check their cash register receipts to see if their bills were correct. Only older people (who had already learned about decimals) would be able to check. The ones who owned stores might use incorrect totals, cheating their customers. The customers would have no way to prove the dishonesty and would have to pay whatever total appeared on bills. The customers would lose money. The dishonest store owners would gain money. Soon older store owners would have a lot of power, because they would have a monopoly on knowledge.

Instant replays

For discipline, one of the most effective techniques I ever stumbled upon is what I called "instant replays." A ninth grader named Dale came into my class late one day, interrupting and announcing loudly, "Sorry, I had to go to the can." Instead of getting mad, chastising him or punishing him—all of which I had tried unsuccessfully in the past—this time I found myself saying calmly, "I think we need an instant replay on that."

I'm not sure why I said it, unless perhaps there had been too much football on television that weekend. At any rate, I continued, saying, "Back up and rewind, Dale. How could you handle that more appropriately?"

To my amazement, Dale actually backed out of the room and came in again, this time tiptoeing, and whispering, in an excessively polite manner, "I am so sorry for being late, Mrs. Thurston." I told him that was much better, but asked for more suggestions for improvement from the group. Someone pointed out that his apology still interrupted the class, and someone else suggested he should have slipped in quietly and apologized and explained to me later. Dale actually listened. The next time he was late, he slipped quietly into the room. The instant replay had given him some attention, which is probably what he most needed and wanted, but it also gave him an alternative to his disruptive behavior.

Always doing it with a sense of humor, I tried using the instant replay routine with other disruptive students, and I usually found that the technique was more effective than anything else I had ever tried. It also worked well in other situations. For example, a pet peeve of mine is a class groaning when I say, "Get out a piece of paper," or "Open your book," or anything that indicates some serious work might be coming up. I believe such behavior sets a negative tone and is, furthermore, unfair because the students have no idea what it is I have planned. Sometimes it is something I know they will enjoy, and their groaning makes me inclined to do something much less pleasant.

The first time the groaning occurs in a class, I explain my position. From then on, if a group forgets and starts groaning, I simply say, "Oops. Instant replay." The kids sit up straight, put angelic looks on their faces, and say, with exaggerated politeness, "Yes, Mrs. Thurston. Right away, Mrs. Thurston." It's a game, and they are teasing, but that's all right. It works. I get over my irritation with them, and they go on to start whatever we are doing with a more positive attitude.

Cheryl Thurston

Romeo, Romeo, like wherefore art thou, like, hiding out

When a class is studying *Romeo and Juliet*, English teachers sometimes have their students rewrite a scene from the play, using contemporary English and modern slang. To do that, students are forced to delve into the play and to understand the sometimes difficult language of Shakespeare. It is not an easy task, but it is one that usually brings both

laughter and understanding into the classroom, particularly when students reenact their scenes. The exercise is an example of the following very effective classroom strategy:

Have students rewrite material in a new form.

When students have to write, they have to think. Don't make the mistake of thinking that writing belongs only in English classes. It can be used effectively in any class, from music and science to art and physical education. It is especially useful for material that you really want students to learn well. To put material into a new form, students must first have a basic understanding of the material. If their understanding is weak, the translating process will force them to clarify what they don't understand. If they already understand the material, the exercise will help reinforce what they have learned. An enjoyable by-product of the rewriting process is, of course, the laughter that

comes with students stretching their minds and imaginations.

Below are just a few ideas for rewriting, from a number of subject areas. Although they might not be appropriate for your specific situation, perhaps they will help you come up with some challenges that are perfect for your students.

History
Rewrite the Gettysburg Address as if spoken by a teenager, a specific political candidate, an eight-year-old child or some other character.

Science
As Elvis Presley, explain photosynthesis to the class.

Arithmetic
Pretend you are a revival preacher. Explain how to multiply fractions.

Government
Create a "rap" song explaining the Bill of Rights.

> "Laugh and the world laughs with you,
> Weep and you weep alone;
> For the sad old earth must borrow its
>   mirth,
> But has trouble enough of its own."
>
> **Ella Wheeler Wilcox**

Geography

In modern slang, explain what monsoons are.

Biology

In a Top Ten List from "Late Show with David Letterman" explain the difference between amphibians and mammals.

Art

As Mr. Rogers or Captain Kangaroo, explain to six-year-olds the difference between complementary and monochromatic color schemes.

Physical education

Create a public service message that will remind children of the basic rules for safe swimming.

Home economics

As Arnold Schwarzenegger, explain how to select a healthy diet, using the basic food pyramid.

Reading

Put the plot of a book you just read into a picture book of 36 pages or less.

Driver's education

Create a nursery rhyme to help you remember the shapes and meanings of traffic signs.

Hunter safety

As an old-fashioned southern belle, explain how to clean a gun.

Youngsterisms

Retired teacher Harold Dunn has coined the term "youngsterisms" in his book *The World According to Kids!* (Spectacle Lane Press, 1992). Dunn had the foresight to write down the funny things his pupils said or wrote, and other teachers, aware of his hobby, also saved items for him. Some of the children's gems over the years:

- A square is a circle with corners.

- An ancestor is an extinct relative.

- Income tacks are the most expensive kind.

Every teacher finds such gems on tests, in papers and in class discussions. Consider following Dunn's lead and start your own file of youngsterisms. Perhaps some day you will wind up with a book, too.

The following exercise is an example of an assignment that has students put material into a new form. It is taken from a unit on the study of slang in English.

★ Say it in slang

Read the following version of *The Emperor's New Clothes*, written in the kind of slang popular in the late sixties and early seventies:

The Emperor's New Clothes

Once upon a time this real cool dude, who was the head honcho of this kingdom, had a real thing about his threads. The dude really grooved on wearing out of sight clothes. He spent a ton of time just changing his duds.

Well, one day these two guys blew into town. They said they were real pros at weaving and could weave real funky stuff, psychedelic stuff that was really out of sight. The thing was, the cloth really was out of sight to some people, or so they said. "Only people with a lot upstairs can see the beauty of our cloth," said the two guys. "Airheads can't. To anyone stupid, the cloth will be invisible."

The king got real hyped up and ordered some of the cloth for himself. The two guys got busy right off. First, they asked for bread to buy the finest silk and gold thread. The king gave it to them, but instead of buying thread, they slipped the dough into their backpacks. Then they pretended to weave, standing by the spinning wheels and pulling imaginary thread through the air.

The king kept sending his aides to check out the guys and see what they were doing. Each aide stuck his nose in and was freaked out to see nothing. Not wanting anyone to think he was a space case, each aide went back to the king and lied. "The stuff's really far out," each reported.

Finally the king decided to bop on over and see for himself. "Dig it?" smiled one of the weavers. "Isn't it out of sight?"

"Yesssssssss," said the king, who was really flipping out. He took a deep breath to calm himself and said, "I mean, well, of course! It's heavy stuff! Boss! Real nifty! I want you to make me some new threads out of it right away. Then I can wear them in the parade day after tomorrow."

"No sweat," said the weavers. "We'll need more bread, and then we'll get right on it."

The king gave them more cash, which they again stuck in their packs. They began pretending to cut and sew the invisible cloth. They really got into it, putting on quite a show. At last, they said they were ready and called the king.

"I can't believe these clothes!" cried the king. "I love them!" Of course he was lying. He nervously stripped down to his skivvies and let the weavers pretend to dress him in the new duds.

(continued)

When the people saw the king parading down the street in nothing but his undies, they freaked. They didn't want anyone to think they were stupid, so they clapped and cheered and said, "Far out! Right on! Groovy! Out of sight!" The king smiled proudly, happy to see what sharp subjects he had.

But at last one little squirt turned to his father and said very loudly, "Hey, Dad. That guy ain't got nothin' on!" Everyone was shocked, but they knew this little kid wasn't stupid. After all, he was the only first grader in the kingdom to have a perfect report card. Everyone began whispering, repeating what the kid had said. Soon everyone was shouting, "The king ain't got nothin' on!"

The king turned bright red, from head to toe. At last he saw that he had been ripped off.

The two weaving dudes split and lived happily ever after.

Find out how a fairy tale might sound in today's slang. Using any kind of modern-day slang (of the good, clean variety), write your own slang version of a popular fairy tale and share it with the class. Here are a few of the fairy tales you might consider rewriting: *Hansel and Gretel, Rapunzel, Little Red Riding Hood, Sleeping Beauty, Three Billy Goats Gruff, Cinderella, Snow White and the Seven Dwarfs, Rumpelstiltskin.*

Review the fairy tale you have chosen by recalling it with other class members or checking in a book of fairy tales. Then write your first draft, including as much slang as you can in your story.

from *Ideas That Really Work!* (Cottonwood Press, Inc.)

A picture is worth a thousand words

A wonderful, caring seventh grade teacher we know had a brilliant young student who adored him. One day she turned in an English composition that was terrible, showing little care or thought in preparation. The teacher simply drew a beautiful turkey at the top of the page and handed it back to the girl, ungraded.

She laughed. She got the point. She started over and turned in a paper that was worthy of her talent.

Certainly such a response by a teacher would be appropriate in only a very few isolated circumstances. However, it does illustrate just one example of the next idea for using humor in the classroom:

Draw pictures — and have your students draw pictures.

You don't have to be an artist to have some fun with pictures. (Be sure to see "Drawing Drips," page 66.) Here are just a few ideas:

- Have students create a "public service" comic strip that gives a clear message related to your subject. For example, a comic strip for a driver's education class could stress that drivers should "Remember the blind spot." A health class comic strip could urge readers to "Limit your intake of sugar and fats." An English class comic strip could show that "Proper spelling and punctuation help increase communication." A comic strip for a government class could give the message, "Apathy is a dangerous thing."

> **"When humor goes, there goes civilization."**
> **Erma Bombeck**

It is a good idea to talk about devices that cartoonists use first. Some examples:

Also talk about how cartoon styles differ (realistic and detailed like "Prince Valiant," distorted like "The Simpsons," etc.). Point out the exaggerations that are often used (large heads, large eyes, tiny legs, etc.). Talk about what makes a cartoon different from a written story or joke (the pictures tell much of the story; dialogue is used extensively; simplicity is important; communication must be crisp and to the point; etc.).

- Draw pictures on your tests. Have a space for students to draw pictures back in response.

- Photocopy a page full of cartoons, but without the dialogue. Have students write captions related to the subject you are studying.

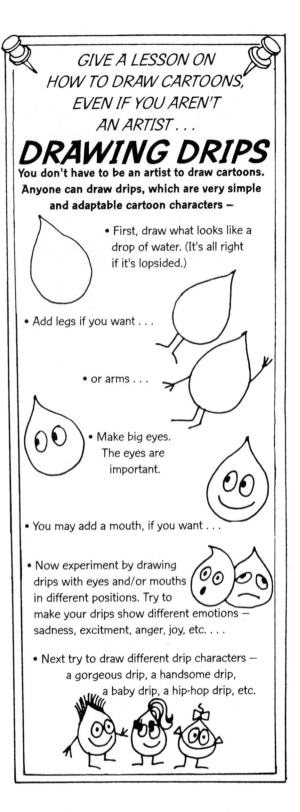

GIVE A LESSON ON HOW TO DRAW CARTOONS, EVEN IF YOU AREN'T AN ARTIST . . .

DRAWING DRIPS

You don't have to be an artist to draw cartoons. Anyone can draw drips, which are very simple and adaptable cartoon characters —

- First, draw what looks like a drop of water. (It's all right if it's lopsided.)

- Add legs if you want . . .

- or arms . . .

- Make big eyes. The eyes are important.

- You may add a mouth, if you want . . .

- Now experiment by drawing drips with eyes and/or mouths in different positions. Try to make your drips show different emotions — sadness, excitment, anger, joy, etc. . . .

- Next try to draw different drip characters — a gorgeous drip, a handsome drip, a baby drip, a hip-hop drip, etc.

Evolution is evolution is evolution . . .

Something similar has happened to nearly every teacher. Suddenly the scheduling doesn't turn out right, and you — with your degree in art history — have to teach a class in biology. "Your transcript shows a class called *The Evolution of Modern Art*," your principal tells you. "And evolution is evolution is evolution."

Of course, you find yourself learning very quickly about mitosis and mammals and parameciums. When you have to teach a subject, you learn fast. There's nothing like teaching to help you learn a subject. That's why the next idea is such a useful one:

Let the students do the teaching.

When students have to teach something, they learn. An effective way for students to teach is through skits, mock-commercials, mini-lessons and other presentations. Such activities really get students involved in a subject and are likely to provide laughter as well.

A few examples of the kinds of things you might try:

English

A radical group has almost convinced the school board that *To Kill a Mockingbird* should be banned in your school district. Videotape a five to 10-minute presentation to the school board, explaining some of the positive themes from the book and their value in today's world.

> **"Wrinkles merely indicate where smiles have been."**
>
> **Mark Twain**

Remember that, because they have to sit through so many meetings, the school board members get bored very easily. You will want to be sure that your group keeps their attention with your presentation.

Arithmetic

You are the manager of a fast-food restaurant that is too poor to buy a fancy new cash register. Your employees have to make change the old-fashioned way. Prepare a 15-minute training session for a new employee, teaching him or her to make change and count it back to a customer correctly.

Auto mechanics

The survival of the human race depends upon three teenagers driving a car across the United States to retrieve a life-saving serum. You have 10 minutes to teach them the absolute basics of car maintenance for their trip, and in a way that is sure to be effective. Remember, the survival of the human race depends upon their success.

History

Suppose that Thomas Jefferson is running for president this year and that you are his campaign manager. Create a one-minute television commercial and a half-page newspaper ad, "selling" your man. Who is Thomas Jefferson? Why should people vote for him?

Social studies

Prepare a "Sesame Street" spot that will teach six-year-olds the importance of the First Amendment.

Science

What is gravity? You have five minutes to explain it to a group of English-speaking aliens who have landed on earth. They have the power to get rid of gravity on this planet, and they figure they might as well, since they don't know what it is. Teach them quickly, and convince them to keep it around.

There's the retarded teacher!

When I was teaching special education, it was sometimes embarrassing to run into children from my school in the supermarket or at the mall. Invariably, I would hear a boy or girl shout across the store, "Hey, look. There's the retarded teacher from my school!"

I preferred to call myself a special ed teacher. However, even that had its disadvantages. When my son David was about four, I brought him to school with me to visit the special ed classes I had been talking about. He interacted with each child at some point during the day and seemed very interested in both the activities and the children. On the ride home, I asked him if he had any questions about my class.

"Just one," he said. "Which one was Ed?"

Elaine Lundberg

68

The best ice cream in the world — Häagen Dazs coffee chip

Most teachers who give spelling tests have found ways to ease the excruciating dullness of the task — dull from the teacher's point of view, at least. You must say a word, use it in a sentence, then wait for the students to write. Then say another word, use it in a sentence, and wait for the students to write.

One teacher eased the boredom one day by mentioning in a sentence that Häagen Dazs coffee chip ice cream is the best ice cream in the universe. Then, in the next sentence, she managed to mention Häagen Dazs coffee chip ice cream again. She was hooked. She had to see if she could make Häagan Dazs coffee chip ice cream a part of each sentence in the test. She did, and she started a tradition. For each spelling test after that, the students chose a theme. The teacher had to make all sentences in the test related to that theme. Thus, the teacher was challenged, and so were the students. She understood that the following idea can be useful in any classroom:

Have some fun with your tests.

Test-taking does not have to be a grim, humorless affair. It is perfectly possible to have a test with serious intent, but in a package that allows for smiles and amusement. Humor and seriousness of purpose are not mutually exclusive.

There are many techniques for adding amusement, spice and interest to your tests. Here are just a few:

- Include trivia questions on your test. The questions might be about odd facts or interesting pieces of information that have been shared in class. Examples: What was the name of Mr. Armstrong's pet boa constrictor in college? What very successful author of children's books was initially rejected by at least two dozen publishers? (Dr. Seuss.) Who invented the bifocal lens? (Benjamin Franklin.)

Some trivia questions might be totally unrelated to anything at all that has come up in class. They might be related to the time of year, to a subject you are about to begin studying, or to just general knowledge. Examples: In the book, *The Grinch Who Stole Christmas*, what was the name of the Grinch's dog? (Max.) What state in the U.S. is closest to what used to be the Soviet Union? (Alaska.) What was Richard Nixon's middle name? (Milhous.)

> **"There are three things which are real: God, human folly and laughter. The first two are beyond our comprehension. So we must do what we can with the third."**
>
> **John F. Kennedy**

- Use students' names. If you are writing a math story problem, give characters the names of students in your class. If students must punctuate a sentence correctly, make the sentence about someone in the class. If you use a hypothetical example in a science or history test, use the names of students in the example. If you must give the same test to several different classes, it is easy to use a computer to make different versions of the test, with different names for each period.

  Note: It is a very good idea to keep track of the students whose names you use, checking their names in your grade book and trying to use everyone's name during the course of a semester. If you don't make a note, it is very easy to lose track and forget which students have already been mentioned. Also, be careful not to use the names of unpopular kids in any way that might be used for unkind teasing.

- Throw in jokes or cartoons or funny drawings. (Here's a good time to refer to your humor therapy log. See page 17.) Another idea is to cut out the dialogue in cartoons and replace it with your own, using students' names.

- Include a goofy question or two that will allow students to be creative or funny in their responses. Examples:

  What is the most boring thing about the Middle Ages? What makes it boring? If you support your answer with convincing detail, you may receive up to five points extra credit.

  If you had the power to eliminate one punctuation mark from all publications written in English from this day forward, what mark would it be? Why? What might be the results of your move?

  If you could cross one amphibian with one insect, what animal would you create? Name and describe your animal and its characteristics.

  What is the best number? Why?

  Give three reasons why a picture of this class should appear in *Newsweek*.

  How would the world be different if humans — and not birds — could fly?

The following is a copy of an actual English test used with ninth graders. It is a test that does the job yet doesn't take itself too seriously. Both the pictures and the content drew many smiles from the students who took it.

Name _____

VOCABULARY TEST

Matching

_____ 1. sallow
_____ 2. morbid
_____ 3. innovation
_____ 4. garrulous
_____ 5. panacea
_____ 6. pseudonym
_____ 7. potpourri
_____ 8. eloquent
_____ 9. zealous
_____ 10. effervescent
_____ 11. melancholy
_____ 12. countenance
_____ 13. tenacious
_____ 14. superlative
_____ 15. nuptials
_____ 16. fallacy
_____ 17. synopsis
_____ 18. plausible
_____ 19. ambiguous
_____ 20. befuddled

a. bubbly; lively
b. superior to others
c. a wedding ceremony
d. love at first sight
e. a change; a new idea or way of doing things
f. miscellaneous collection
g. gruesome
h. twosome
i. vivid, expressive in speech or writing
j. persistent, stubborn
k. brief summary
l. pen name; false name
m. jolly
n. jelly
o. peanut butter
p. confused; perplexed
q. supposed remedy for all ills
r. not clear; having more than one mean ing
s. facial expression
t. sad, depressed
u. seemingly true; believable
v. yellowish; unhealthy-looking
w. talkative
x. a mistaken idea; a flaw in reasoning
y. unbelievable
z. intensely enthusiastic

Pictures for your viewing pleasure:

Fill in the Blank

A LOVE STORY

Once upon a time there was a kingdom that had a _____ king, the best king in the whole world. He had a son he wanted to marry off. The son was not very healthy-looking. He had a _____ complexion and his _____ always wore a frown.

One day the king got up to speak to his subjects. He was so _____ that the people were spellbound. He announced a contest, offering his son's foot in marriage to the young woman who could slay the dragon that lived outside the castle walls. "She must kill the dragon by Wednesday," said the king. "Then the _____ and reception will be on Thursday."

(continued)

(continued)

Now there happened to be only one young woman in the kingdom who even wanted the prince. This lady, however, was quite _____ in her efforts to win him. She watched the dragon day and night, trying to find the best way to slay him. She became so preoccupied with killing him that her mother began to worry. "Your thoughts are becoming positively _____," she said. "It's not healthy."

Still, the princess was _____, refusing to give up her gruesome goal. She collected a _____ of different weapons to use on the dragon. Then she set out for the kill.

Quietly, she approached the dragon. Suddenly, he lifted his head and looked at her. "Hi, there!" he said.

The princess was startled. "Uh, hi," she said.

What do you think of the Broncos?" asked the dragon. Before she could answer, he began chattering away about football.

The princess was surprised. She hadn't expected the dragon to be so _____. In fact, she hadn't expected him to talk at all. She didn't know dragons could talk, and she couldn't understand how he could do that. She was _____. She decided to get on with her mission. She drew her sword. The dragon started talking about the Dallas Cowboys. She got out her gun. The dragon talked about the Miami Dolphins. She got out a slingshot. The dragon talked about the Chicago Bears.

The princess was bored silly by all the football talk. In fact, she was bored into inaction and finally just dropped off to sleep.

When she woke up, the dragon was gone. Frowning, she got up. She felt _____ that she hadn't killed him.

The princess did not win the prince's foot in marriage. Unfortunately, they did not live happily ever after.

Sword

Princess

Dragon's tail
(clever illustrating trick
for people who can't draw dragons)

Sometimes tests don't have to be for students. You might try the following just-for-fun teacher test at a department meeting or in the teachers' lounge:

★ Teacher burn-out test

Teacher burn-out is a growing problem nationwide. Do you suspect that you might be suffering from a case? If so, simply answer yes or no to each of the questions below:

_____ Do you find yourself lugging home a briefcase full of papers and lugging them back to school, without ever opening the case?

_____ Do you feel frustrated because you can't afford a briefcase?

_____ Have you stopped feeling grateful for the free canvas book tote you got at a convention last fall?

_____ Has your principal ever found a resume you left behind in the copy machine?

_____ Does the word sabbatical send an adrenaline rush through your body?

_____ Have you found yourself arriving at school in your bedroom slippers?

_____ Do you correct misspellings on thank-you notes from friends, in red pen?

_____ Do you find yourself getting angry that high school students are driving nicer cars than you are?

_____ Have you ever purposely scraped the side of a student's 1996 Camaro Z–28 with your 1974 Dodge Colt?

_____ Does chalk dust bring on a migraine headache?

_____ Do you coach sports you hate because you need the extra $200?

_____ Have you grown fond of the school's tuna surprise?

_____ Do you daydream about becoming an independent electrician or a real estate agent?

_____ Do you daydream about saying, "Would you like fries with that, sir?"

_____ Has going to the bathroom whenever you wanted started to seem like the ultimate in job perks?

(continued)

(continued)

_____ Have you occasionally found yourself not caring about a student's self-esteem, particularly if he's pulling a knife on someone?

_____ Have you ever absent-mindedly signed your check with a smiley face?

_____ Do you secretly cheer inside when there's an unscheduled fire drill, just so you can get out of class for a while?

_____ Do you sometimes set off the fire alarm when no one is looking?

_____ Have you ever drawn a mustache on the superintendent's picture in the school yearbook?

_____ Have you ever marked an "X" where you should have marked a "\" on the attendance card — on purpose?

_____ Have you ever found yourself screaming obscenities at the sound of the intercom coming on, again?

_____ Have you stopped reading memos from the office?

_____ Have you ever stayed home sick and not sent in lesson plans for the substitute?

_____ Have you ever lost your entire class on the way to an assembly?

_____ Have you ever attended an educational convention and not attended one meeting?

_____ Have you ever just arbitrarily made up grades for report cards, rather than add up points and figure averages?

_____ Has your grandmother died more than once this school year?

Scoring

Give yourself one point for every "yes" answer. Then take the following actions, depending upon your score.

0 - 5:	You are either a student teacher or Mother Theresa. Burn-out is not a problem.
5 -10:	You are showing early warning signs of teacher burn-out. If you don't know the difference between psychiatrists, psychotherapists, psychologists and counselors, start learning.
11-20:	You need to apply for a sabbatical. NOW.
21-25:	You are suffering full-blown teacher burn-out. Make sure your spouse is gainfully employed.
Over 26:	Contact Forest Lawn. Ask about teacher discounts.

Even teachers get the blahs

If, over the years, you have taught children how to divide decimals at least a hundred and seventy times, it is possible that you might occasionally be just a tad bored teaching how to divide decimals. If you have taught comma rules every November for 26 years, it is not surprising if one November you wake up and feel you just can't look at a comma ever again. Every teacher gets the "blahs"

once in a while. If you find yourself bored or in a rut, try this suggestion:

Take a risk.

Taking a risk can sometimes jolt you, and a class, out of a case of the doldrums. You might know exactly how students will react when you get to Problem #4 on page 227 of your textbook, but you may not know how they will react if you try something really different. If you take a risk, a real risk, you have got to be on your toes, for you don't know what will happen. You will also be very likely to run into some laughter, as you and your students are surprised by something different.

> **"Even professional comedians don't know if their humor will work until they try it, and sometimes it doesn't."**
>
> **Esther Blumenfeld and Lynne Alpern**

Here are just a few risk-taking ideas:

- Do something unexpected. Examples: If you always have students work alone, try small groups for a day. Lead an aerobics class using "Sesame Street" songs or gospel music, instead of popular tunes. Look at popular music of this century instead of battles during history class. Snap photographs of students as they take a test, just for the fun of it. If you never have group discussions, have a group discussion, no matter what you teach.

  If you always have group discussions, try a lecture. If you are playing baseball in gym class, have everyone skip instead of run for two innings. Shave your mustache. Wear a blonde wig to school. Read aloud something you love, for no other reason than you love it.

- Try "Let's-see-what-will-happen-if experiments." For example, a language arts teacher might say, "Let's see what will happen if we don't use any spoken language at all this period, only writing." The experiment may lead to some interesting insights into the strengths and limits of spoken language vs. written language. It might also lead to a new understanding of the importance of spelling, punctuation and clarity in written communication.

  When a class is studying plant growth, a science teacher might say, "Let's see what will happen if we plant seeds in all kinds of things collected from around the house — dryer lint, oatmeal, tea bags, grass clippings, etc." In a lesson on slang, an English teacher might say, "Let's see what will happen if we make up our own slang word for 'Darn!' and start using it in this school." An arithmetic teacher might say, "Let's see what will happen if we try to eliminate all numbers from our classroom for an entire day."

The danger of what-will-happen-if experiments is that you don't know what will happen, or even if anything will happen at all. They are a risk, but when they work, they are thought-provoking, interesting and a lot of fun.

- Ask a real question, one to which you don't know the answer. Examples: If Benjamin Franklin could meet Supreme Court Justice Sandra Day O'Connor, what might the two say to each other? How would the world be different if the shape "circle" did not exist? What might happen if cows could read? How would holidays be different if girls' volleyball instead of football were played during holiday bowl games?

Two mini-dramas

Mini-dramas can add pizzazz to both the classroom and to real life. Here are examples from both settings:

Classroom drama

One day my seventh grade students and I wound up in a discussion about how people often see what they want to see and hear what they want to hear. We talked about how people tend to remember information that supports their point of view, while filtering out information that does not. We also talked about how even what we see with our own eyes is not always reliable, depending upon the circumstances.

Many students insisted that facts are facts. They had trouble understanding that many factors may influence our judgment and objectivity. So a few days later I staged a mini-drama. I planned the performance with my assistant principal, and without the knowledge of my students.

The next day, as I was teaching class, Mr. Tarket walked into the room and, with his back to the class, began talking to me in a low voice about some forms I was supposed to have filled out. He was clearly angry, but he kept his voice low at all times. At one point, he hit the top of my desk to emphasize a point, and knocked over a vase of flowers on my desk, sending flowers and a bit of water into the first row. Finally, he stormed out. Clearly upset, I went on with class.

The kids were absolutely silent, stunned to see Mr. Tarket yelling at me.

During the classroom break, they found reasons to come up to me. "Your hair looks really nice today, Mrs. Thurston," one girl said. "I like your blouse, Mrs. Thurston," said another. Seeming to want to make contact and see if I was all right, they asked me silly questions about anything at all. I was touched by their concern — although no one mentioned what had happened.

After the break, I told the students that Mr. Tarket had only been acting. Then I asked them to write down exactly what they had observed during Mr. Tarket's visit. The results were interesting, to say the least. Mr. Tarket was wearing a blue jacket, or a black jacket, or no jacket at all. He was yelling at me, shouting at the top of his lungs at me, or just mumbling to me. He slapped the desk once, or he pounded it numerous times. He knocked over the vase accidentally, or he shoved it on purpose. The water spilled all over a boy in the front row, or it ruined papers on my desk, or it dripped harmlessly on the floor. And I reacted to the whole thing by looking hot, or by getting angry, or by starting to cry.

The students laughed as I read aloud the widely differing accounts of what they had all seen with their own eyes. They began to see that finding the "facts" is not as easy as it seems.

Cheryl Thurston

Dinner drama

Mitch and I reveled in the privacy of a Saturday night dinner at a recession struck restaurant. As the only two patrons, we chatted loudly and took the time to savor each bite of our entrees.

Unfortunately, our intimate meal was invaded. Like ants to a picnic, an obnoxiously boisterous couple found their way through the empty restaurant to the table adjacent to ours. Their bickering smothered our conversation, compelling me to listen in on their fight. Men may not realize this, but a woman can carry on a discussion while totally eavesdropping on others. So, while nodding and uh-huh-ing to Mitch, I overheard the following:

Woman: "I don't want to eat anything."

Man: "Look, I do not take a woman to a nice restaurant to have her watch me eat. You will order something."

The waiter came over to take their order.

Woman: "I'll just have a salad."

Man: "No, she will not just have a salad. I could have taken her to Burger King if she just wanted a salad. I know what the lady likes. I will order for her. She'll have the quail and lentil soup and . . ."

When the waiter left, the woman flipped out.

Woman: "I can't believe you ordered for me! You have some nerve! You just want to get me fat, don't you? That's it. I know you're not attracted to me anymore. I see you looking at other women. You see? You're staring at that girl right now!"

She was right. I got flustered and attempted to feign participation in Mitch's monologue. Their fight escalated until the woman finally screamed, "We've been going out for over two years, you treat me like dirt, and you've been leading me on! You're never going to ask me to marry you!" She got up to leave, but the man grabbed her and forced her to sit.

Man: "Well, I was waiting until later on to do this, but . . ."

He knelt, took out a small box, and said, "Will you marry me?"

While he asked her, he glanced at me. The woman saw this and infuriated, yelled, "I can't believe you! You're even looking at another woman when you're asking me to marry you! You'll never change! There's no way I'd spend the rest of my life with you!"

She threw the box down and ran out. The man chased after her.

Mitch called out, "Hey! You forgot your ring!"

"Forget it! You keep it!" the man answered, while dashing out of the restaurant.

Mitch grabbed the ring, got down on one knee, and said, "Jill, will you marry me?"

"What?! Give them their ring back!" I demanded.

"But, Jill, they said I could have it. C'mon, it's a free ring. Will you marry me?"

I kept telling him that he was crazy. He couldn't use someone else's ring. Then I told him he was being cheap . . .

Mitch continued to genuflect, repeating his question. "This is no joke," he claimed. "I'm serious."

But I wouldn't believe him. He broke down.

"OK, OK. I set the whole thing up! Now, WILL YOU MARRY ME?"

Confused and in shock, I began to laugh. I tried to make my mouth form an answer, but my brain wouldn't cooperate. So I cried.

The waiter appeared, script in hand, and said, "You're supposed to say 'yes.'"

"Yes! Yes! I will!" I blurted, and then laughed and cried simultaneously. Mitch stared, unsure whether it was safe to kiss me yet. Soon, the acting couple and the entire restaurant joined him, all carrying their scripts.

Mitch wrote the whole skit, even the waiter's question about which salad dressing the woman wanted. He got two people to perform the "play," informed the entire restaurant staff, and had everyone rehearse there three times before that night. The only thing he didn't do was time it so that I could have finished my food.

Well, I definitely fell for it. Better yet, I fell for a guy that's going to make the rest of my life quite interesting!

Jill Sverdlove
(Reprinted with permission from the *Denver Post*)

Why should I pay the electric bill? I didn't major in math.

So much of the time, schools divide life into categories. We teach about numbers only in math classes, about writing only in English classes, about responsibility only in civics classes and about nutrition only in home economics classes. Naturally, this categorization sometimes gives students an inaccurate picture of the world.

Life is really a "glob" of stuff, without categories of knowledge. That's why it's fun, and useful, to surprise students with this idea:

Mix things up.

Students need to understand that life is not made up of isolated little units that never overlap. When we go to pay our electric bill, for example, we need to use math skills to check its accuracy and to subtract the amount from our checking account. We need to know how to write in order to sign the check. If there's a problem with the bill, we need to use language skills to call and explain the problem clearly. If the electric company refers us to an explanation in a brochure, we need to be able to read and understand that brochure.

> **"It's bad to suppress laughter. It goes back down and spreads to your hips."**
>
> **Fred Allen**

Like life, school should be filled with subjects that mix together and overlap. Surprise your students by mixing things up as often as possible. Humor often comes from the unex-

pected, and so does learning. Here are just a few ideas

- In English class, sing. Have students set a poem to music. Or set a rule to music, and have everyone memorize it by singing it.

- Read aloud a short story during math class, perhaps a mystery that involves a mathematical puzzle or creative problem-solving.

- Dance during history class. Have someone come in and teach students popular dances from this century. Talk about what was happening in the country when each dance was popular.

- Try physical exercise during civics. Have students create a ball game that illustrates different types of government.

- Play with numbers during art. Have students create designs using only correctly-solved multiplication problems.

- Draw during science. Have students create and draw a new kind of mammal, amphibian, reptile, insect, bird or fish.

If students need to remember that life can't be categorized into subject areas, so do teachers. Medicine, for example, is not completely the domain of physicians. Teachers have their own special kind of medical terminology:

★ Medical terminology for teachers

attack: object put on your chair by a student

aphasia: stage teenagers are going through

barium: what the dog did with Julie's science homework

benign: what most fourth graders will be on their birthday

cap or crown: headgear not allowed during class

choke: a funny comment that makes the class laugh

colitus: what your car did to the principal's car in the parking lot

dislocated disc: computer software missing from library

endorphins: small children whose parents never pick them up on time after school

enema: between j-k-l and p

fracture: a portion of, as in 1/3

hangnail: hook in supply closet for coat

incontinent: where Johnny's notebook is

injection: part of speech

joint pain: occurs when a student is caught using drugs in the rest room

kidney stone: rock thrown at a teacher's back during recess

major depression: mark in student's hair, made by baseball cap

pancreas: wrinkles in trousers from sitting for six hours for achievement tests

X-ray: type of magazine hidden in notebooks (*Playboy* and *Penthouse*, for example)

There he goes again . . .

Have you ever watched a child laugh? A little girl may get intense delight out of watching someone pop up from behind a sofa and say, "boo." Furthermore, she will laugh again and again and again at the same stunt. Although there are few adults who find saying "boo" particularly hysterical, most of us will perform for a child, again and again

and again, just to see the child's delight. Furthermore, we will find ourselves laughing along with the child. Because laughter is contagious, the following idea is useful in the classroom:

Share what you think is funny, even if you're the only one who thinks so.

What you find funny depends upon your own personal taste. Your sense of humor has been shaped by your childhood environment, your life experiences and the way you perceive life.

If you persist in sharing what you think is funny, your amusement will sometimes prove catching. Students may start seeing the humor

> **"Analyzing humor is like dissecting a frog. Few people are interested and the frog dies of it."**
>
> **E.B. White**

in elephant jokes or the "Dilbert" comic strip. They may start appreciating Gary Larson's warped cartoons, laughing at Dave Barry's wild exaggerations or smiling at Garrison Keillor's rambling stories about people in Lake Wobegon. Sometimes they will laugh just because smiling and laughter are contagious. Even if no one learns to appreciate what you appreciate, students may find humor in the fact that you could find certain things humorous at all!

Teachers should share what they think is funny with their students. But they also should share with fellow teachers. Perhaps the following diet will give some of your colleagues a lift:

★ Stress diet for teachers

Have you tried many diets over the years, only to find that they don't work for you? Perhaps you haven't been taking into account the special stresses of teaching. The following diet is one that is designed just for teachers. Give it a try. It is sure to be a diet that will fit you and your life style.

Breakfast
1/2 grapefruit
1 slice of whole wheat toast, dry
1 6 oz. carton plain yogurt
4 cups black coffee

Planning period
2 cups black coffee
1 small apple

Lunch
4 oz. lean broiled turkey
lettuce
1/2 tomato
3 low-salt Triscuits
1 diet Coke or iced tea with artificial sweetener
1 Oreo cookie

After-school snack
rest of Oreos in package
1 pint of Ben and Jerry's Cherry Garcia ice cream
1/2 jar hot fudge sauce
nuts, cherries, whipped cream
OR
3 margaritas
1 16 oz. package of nacho-flavored Doritos
salsa
1 can of bean dip

Dinner
1 large sausage, pepperoni and mushroom pizza, extra cheese
1 loaf of garlic bread
4 12 oz. cans of light beer
1 large salad with half a bottle of blue cheese dressing
1 Dove Bar

After-you-have-finished-grading-papers snack
1 entire frozen Sara Lee cheese cake, eaten directly from freezer

(continued)

(continued)

Rules and rationale of stress dieting

1. If you eat something and no one sees you eat it, it has no calories.

2. Tastes from someone else's plate have no calories.

3. If you drink a diet soda with a brownie, the calories in the diet soda will cancel out the calories in the brownie.

4. Foods licked off knives and fingers have no calories, if you are cooking.

5. Potato chips eaten during a PMS attack have no calories. Neither does chocolate.

6. The calories from two scoops of Häagen Dazs spontaneously combust when placed in eight ounces of diet cola.

7. When you eat with someone else, calories don't count if you don't eat more than the other person does.

8. Food eaten for medicinal purposes does not count. Examples: hot chocolate, toast, milk and cookies, mashed potatoes, ice cream, brandy.

9. Movie-related foods do not have calories because they are part of an entire entertainment package and not part of one's personal fuel. This includes Milk Duds, buttered popcorn, gummy bears, Junior Mints and Tootsie Rolls.

10. Tiny slivers cut from a cake have no calories, as long as they are no more than 1/4" wide each.

11. Bites taken while grading papers have no calories.

12. Cookie pieces contain no calories. The process of breaking causes calorie leakage. Similarly, cookie dough has no calories. The process of baking adds them.

13. When eating out, desserts contain no calories, as long as you have black coffee and split the dessert with someone else.

14. Anything consumed while on vacation has no calories.

As long as we are on the topic of food, consider the following recipe. It fits easily into nearly any teacher's diet:

Spam Stroganoff

1 can Spam
1 onion, sliced thin
2 Tbsp. butter
1/2 tsp. salt
1/2 tsp. thyme
1/2 cup sour cream

1 lb. beef tenderloin, sliced in thin strips
1/2 lb. fresh mushrooms, sliced thin
1/2 cup water, or beef stock
1/8 tsp. pepper
1/4 cup dry sherry

In a medium-sized skillet, sauté beef, onion and mushrooms in butter for 2–3 minutes. Add water, salt, pepper and thyme; simmer, covered 20–30 minutes. While it is simmering, take the unopened can of Spam and put it away in the cupboard. Add sherry and sour cream to beef mixture, and serve over rice.

Serving suggestions: the can of Spam can also be placed in the center of the table, as a stark reminder of what you could be eating. Many people might think this dish is costly; it's actually very economical, since you can use the same can of Spam again and again.

Why isn't anyone laughing?

I was in the post office one day, waiting in line with a lot of people. We all heard one of the postal clerks turn to the other and say, "What's Bob's last name?" The other clerk answered, "Bob who?"

I started laughing. Everyone looked at me strangely. Another time, I was standing in line at a diner and cracked up when I looked up at the posted menu, which listed the dinner specials:

Turkey sandwich $4.95
French Dip sandwich $5.95
Fish and chips $5.95
Children $1.95

"How much are kids going for a pound?" I asked. Again, everyone looked at me strangely.

Or recently I was giving a workshop, and the woman next door to me was giving a pet bird behavior seminar. Bird behavior? A seminar? The participants didn't understand why I started laughing when I saw their flyer.

My son, however, saves me. I tell him the stories about what has made me laugh. Sometimes he thinks my stories are stupid, but by the time I finish telling them and retelling them, he laughs. He laughs, he's 19, and he's never been convicted. What a great son!

Elaine Lundberg

Would you like fries with that, sir?

For teenagers who aspire to lives of comfort and wealth, a career at the counter of McDonald's or Wendy's is probably not going to meet their needs. We know some parents who never lecture when their teenagers bring home less-than-spectacular report cards or otherwise fail to meet expectations. They simply look at the kids and say, "Would you like fries with that, sir?" The parents are modeling what they hope their children do *not* wind up doing for a career. Teachers also can often teach a valuable lesson with the same approach:

Demonstrate what *not* to do.

A speaker who was to address a ninth grade civics class met the teacher outside the door just after the bell rang. He spent a few moments putting his clothes in disarray. He loosened his tie, stuffed one pants cuff into his shoe, messed up his hair, and unbuttoned one shirt cuff. He had the teacher go in and apologize for the speaker's tardiness. Then, in a few minutes, he walked into the room.

> **"Blessed are we who can laugh at ourselves, for we shall never cease to be amused."**
>
> **Unknown**

He spoke softly. He looked to the side of the room, avoiding the students' eyes. He mumbled. He hemmed and hawed. He acted very uncertain.

Soon the students were casting sidelong glances at one another and rolling their eyes. He had lost them. They began whispering among themselves and writing notes.

Suddenly the speaker stood up straight, straightened his tie, started speaking clearly, and demanded the students' attention, simply by his manner and tone of voice. "You have one chance to make a first impression," he said. "And what you just saw is how *not* to act on a job interview." Very effectively, he had made his point.

Demonstrating what not to do is often funny and instructive as well. For example, one college instructor hands out detailed instructions for "How not to pass freshmen writing." Students always laugh, but they get the message. Another shows how not to address an audience for a speech. She cracks her gum, lounges against the podium and goes off on tangents like this:

That was last Tuesday . . . wait. No, it was the day I had to pick up the dry cleaning, which was on Wednesday. I remember because it was the same day I had to take the cat to the vet. He had been throwing up all day, I think it was the remains of an old can of tuna he had dug out of the trash. I'd forgotten to dump it the day the trash guys come, so it had gotten pretty rank. I always have trouble remembering to take the trash out, for some reason. Maybe it's because my ex-husband always used to do it. I never even had to think about it. Anyway, where was I? Oh, yes. I was talking about last Tuesday, I mean Wednesday . . .

Again, the students understand.

There is, however, danger in demonstrating what not to do. The incorrect image is sometimes what students remember most. It is very important, therefore, to follow up a negative demonstration with a positive one, showing the correct way to do things. That way the contrast will be more vivid, and students are more likely to remember what they *should* remember.

There were three inmates on death row. They had been together for five years and had been telling the same nine jokes over and over again. Then the prison instituted a new policy, allowing prisoners only fifteen minutes to socialize each day. One of the inmates suggested that they number the jokes from one to nine, to save time, and the others readily agreed.

The next day, the first convict said, "Joke number four!" The other two started laughing uproariously. The next convict said, "Joke number seven!" The other two laughed so hard tears came to their eyes. Finally, the last convict shouted, "Joke number two!"

There was silence.

Again he shouted, "Joke number two!"

Again, silence.

"What's wrong?" shouted the convict, exasperated. "Joke number two is a really funny joke!"

"Not the way you tell it," replied the first convict.

The following "what not to do" exercise is effective for nearly any class. Before giving the test, mention that some students may already have taken a similar test at some time. (There are a number of different versions around.) Stress that those students are not to say anything, but to go ahead and complete the test again, sitting quietly when finished.

Most students will rush through the test, completing the items that tell them to shout, hum, draw, add, subtract, etc. After the time is up, see if anyone really did follow the instructions and complete only items #1, #2, and #3.

Name _____

★ Following Instructions: A Test

This is a test on following instructions. You will have exactly ten minutes to complete it. Be sure to read all of the items below, #1–#25, before you begin.

1. Write your name at the top of this paper, in the space provided.
2. Draw a star after your name.
3. Sign your name at the bottom, center, of this page.
4. Draw a hat on the face in the left-hand margin.
5. Write the alphabet in small letters, across the top of this page.
6. Divide 786 by 2. Put the answer here: _____
7. Softly hum the tune to "Row, Row, Row Your Boat" as you complete item #8.
8. Draw horizontal stripes in the triangle in the right-hand margin.
9. Add your zip code to the year you were born. Put the answer here:
10. If you get this far, repeat these words aloud, three times: "One-third finished!"
11. Draw a heart inside the box in the right-hand margin.
12. What is your favorite color? _____
13. Turn around and smile at the person seated behind you. If no one is seated behind you, smile at your teacher.
14. Write down the name of any teacher you had last year: _____
15. Spell out your last name, backwards. _____
16. Stand up and stretch. You deserve a break.
17. Which do you like better, dogs or cats? _____
18. Draw a tiny circle in the bottom, right-hand corner of this page.
19. What is your favorite television program? _____
20. Write down the seventh, fourteenth, and twenty-third letters of the alphabet:_____
21. If you get this far, shout these words, twice: "I'm going to finish on time!"
22. Turn this page over and draw a large house.
23. If the house you drew doesn't have a chimney, draw one, with smoke coming out of it.
24. Subtract 39 from 2567. Write the answer here: _____
25. Complete only items #1, #2, and #3 above. Ignore items #4—#24.

Reprinted from *Ideas that Really Work!* (Cottonwood Press, Inc.)

The following exercise is an example of a lesson that demonstrates both what to do and what not to do.

★ With slang; without slang

If you are frustrated by your students' speech habits, you are not alone. It seems that many young people are unable to get a sentence out of their mouths without using a great deal of slang and throwing in "like" and "you know" every few words. To show students that speech habits do make a difference, try the following exercise.

First choose some students to rehearse the following interviews and perform them before the class. You will need the following characters: Talk Show Host, Author #1 and Author #2. Author #1 and Author #2 may be played by the same person.

Conversation #1

Talk Show Host: I'd like to introduce our next guest, Lila Harrington, who is here to tell us about her new book, *American Schools Today*. Welcome, Ms. Harrington.

Author #1: Hi.

Host: Can you tell us why you wrote your book, Ms. Harrington?

Author #1: Sure. Well, see, like it was a couple a years ago and I was, like, teaching in a school, a junior high. I was, you know, like really gettin' into it — teaching, I mean. Then, see, one day I read this article about all the bad stuff going on in schools — you know, like drugs and violence and kids not learning nothing, and stuff like that. And I'm like, "That's not *my* school." So I go, "You know, like maybe I ought to write a book." So, like, I did!

Host: I see. And what is your book about, exactly?

Author #1: Well, it's about, like, good stuff, you know, good stuff going on in schools. It gives you a real good picture of kids today.

Host: And how do your students feel about the book?

Author #1: They're like, "Wow! Ms. Harrington! That's like so cool!" They're really like blown away that I'd do something like that.

Host: I'm afraid we have to go now, Ms. Harrington. Thank you for speaking with us today.

Author #1: Thanks a lot. And I guess that means I'm outta here!

(continued)

(continued)

Conversation #2

Talk Show Host: I'd like to introduce our next guest, Lila Harrington, who is here to tell us about her new book, *American Schools Today*. Welcome, Ms. Harrington.

Author #2: Thank you.

Host: Can you tell us why you wrote your book, Ms. Harrington?

Author #2: Yes. Two or three years ago, I was teaching at a junior high and really enjoying it. Then one day I read a newspaper article about all the negative things happening in schools today — drugs, violence and so little learning taking place. I found myself thinking, "That's not my school." I knew a lot of very positive things were going on in my school, and in schools where my friends taught. So I came up with the idea of writing a book myself.

Host: I see. And what is your book about, exactly?

Author #2: It's about all the positive things that are happening in schools today. I wanted to show the world a more optimistic view of education.

Host: And how do your students feel about the book?

Author #2: They think it's wonderful. They are so impressed that one of their own teachers would write a book, and a book about them.

Host: I'm afraid we have to go now, Ms. Harrington. Thank you for speaking with us today.

Author #2: Thank you for inviting me.

Reprinted from *Ideas That Really Work!* (Cottonwood Press, Inc.)

Happiness is seeing your principal's picture on a milk carton

Some teachers can't get along with their school principal. Some can't get along with other teachers. Some can't get along with the custodian or a certain parent or someone else. In any school, in any given week, dozens of tense situations occur, some more serious than others, but often involving personalities at odds with one another. Try the following tip for coping:

Use humor to help diffuse tension.

Humor can help put problems into perspective. It can distract and allow time for tempers to calm. It can help soothe hurt feelings or embarrassment.

Suppose, for example, that someone throws up in an assembly. It won't do any good to act as if the incident never happened. Instead, you might later say, "That reminds me of one of my most embarrassing moments." Then matter-of-factly share a story about a personal embarrassment, and invite others to do the same. The embarrassed student is likely to feel less humiliation after others have shared and laughed about similar stories.

If another teacher's long, drawn-out complaints at teachers' meetings are driving you crazy, twist your irritation into amusement. Predict to yourself what the person will complain about next, or guess the number of complaints or the length of time he or she will waste during the meeting. You can have a secret laugh when your predictions come true. As the complainer speaks, jot down exaggerated, imagined responses, to put the person in his or her place. Doodle your own private caricature of the complainer,

or keep a running log of ridiculous quotations from the complainer. Turning your anger into amusement can be an enormous tension release.

When tempers flare, it helps if you keep yours in line. A light-hearted remark in a tense

> **"Then I commended mirth, because a man hath no better thing under the sun, than to eat, and to drink, and to be merry."**
> **Ecclesiastes VIII**

situation can keep a problem from escalating. One third grade teacher has a "what-if" discussion when two children are starting to fight. She sits them down and starts listing a string of far-fetched possibilities that could result from their actions. She might say something like this:

"Now what if you really did hit him? Suppose you broke his nose, and he

started bleeding. You know how the sight of blood makes me sick. What if I got dizzy and fainted, and they had to call 911, and the emergency medical team came rushing in here, and the television crews were following because a school emergency would make such good news, and then they got here, and all they found was this teacher on the ground who fainted at the sight of some blood? How embarrassing! I would look like a wimp on the 5:00 o'clock news, with everyone watching, and it would be all your fault!"

Her exaggerations usually work. The students calm down, smile or start to giggle, and she is able to go on to help them deal with their problem constructively.

People are amazing in their resourcefulness. Two Colorado women have used humor to help them in their fights against cancer. Undergoing chemotherapy, both lost their hair. Undaunted, one attended a Halloween party as Ghandi and won the costume contest. Another, a teacher, went to a costume store and bought a collection of outrageous wigs. She would appear before her junior high students one day in a Cleopatra wig, another day in a Shirley Temple curls, another day in a giant Afro, another day in a white, Martha Washington-style wig. Her sense of humor helped both her and her students cope with her illness.

At last report, by the way, both women are doing just fine.

Knotty, knotty

When a group needs a tension reliever, try playing "Knotty, Knotty." Have students get into groups of eight. (Or have one group at a time participate, while the others watch.) Students should stand shoulder-to-shoulder, in a circle. Each student must then take the hands of two group members not standing next to him or her. Each student will thus end up holding hands with two other students. Then instruct the group to unwind so that they are again standing in a circle but without letting go of each other's hands. The group will wind up twisting, stepping over linked arms, and managing to get into all kinds of contortions as they try to untwist their group knot. It can be done, of course, but not without some cooperation and a lot of laughter.

Other ideas?

The ideas in this book have worked for us or for people we know, and we hope that at least some of them will work for you. We are sure that many of you will have other good ideas that are not included in these pages. If so, we sincerely hope you will write and tell us about them, for we would like to update this book regularly. How do you use humor effectively in the classroom? What activities have been particularly successful in your classroom at inspiring both laughter and learning? What funny experiences and stories can you share? (Of course, we will give you credit for any material we use.)

Just write to us in care of Cottonwood Press, Inc.; 305 West Magnolia, Suite 398; Fort Collins, Colorado 80521.

In the meantime, we wish you health, happiness, fun and laughter — in both your classroom and in your life!

Cheryl Thurston
Elaine Lundberg

Bibliography

Barnhart, Nikki C. "Humor: An Art in Itself." *The Delta Kappa Gamma Bulletin.* Winter 1988: 9+.

Blos, Joan W. "Getting It: The First Notch on the Funny Bone." *SLJ School Library Journal.* May 1979: 38–39.

Bryant, Jennings, Paul W. Comiskey, Jon S. Crane, and Dolf Zillmann. "Relationship Between College Teachers' Use of Humor in the Classroom and Students' Evaluations of Their Teachers." *Journal of Educational Psychology.* 72 (1980): 511–519.

Colwell, Clyde G. "Humor as a Motivational and Remedial Technique." *Journal of Reading.* March 1981: 484–486.

Crabbes, Michael A., Susan K. Crabbes, and Joel Goodman. "Giving the Gift of Humor (ho, ho, ho): An Interview with Joel Goodman." *Elementary School Guidance and Counseling.* Dec. 1986: 105–113.

Damico, Sandra Bowman. "What's so Funny about a Crisis? Clowns in the Classroom." *Contemporary Education.* Spring 1980: 131–134.

Davis, Tom. "Humor and Creativity are, at Least, Kissing Cousins." *Course Trends.* Oct. 1989–4.

Fadiman, Clifton. "Humor as a Weapon." *The Center Magazine* (a publication of the Center for the Study of Democratic Institutions). Jan./Feb. 1971.

"A Fantastic Disparity." *The Creative Child and Adult Quarterly.* 5 (1980).

Gallagher, Mary. "Teaching Comedy to Class Comedians." *English Journal.* Feb. 1981: 51–52.

Gentile, Lance M., and Merna M. McMillan. "Humor and the Reading Program." *Journal of Reading.* Jan. 1978: 343–349.

Hageseth, Christian III. *A Laughing Place.* Ft. Collins, CO: Berwick, 1988.

Hickerson, Benny. "The Other Funny Thing in the Classroom . . . Kids." *English Journal.* March 1989: 52–54.

"Humor and the Child." *Contemporary Education.* Spring 1982: 128-131.

Hunsaker, Johanna S. "It's No Joke: Using Humor in the Classroom." *The Clearing House.* Feb. 1988: 285–286.

"The Influence of Humorous Atmosphere on Divergent Thinking." *Contemporary Educational Psychology.* 8 (1983): 68–75.

Klasky, Charles. "Some Funny Business in Your Reading Classes." *Journal of Reading.* May 1979: 731–733.

Klein, Allen. *The Healing Power of Humor.* Los Angeles: Jeremy P. Tarcher, Inc., 1989.

Leone, Robert E. "Life After Laughter: One Perspective." *Elementary School Guidance and Counseling.* Dec. 1986: 139–142.

Long, Patricia. "Laugh and Be Well?" *Psychology Today.* Oct. 1987: 28–29.

McGee, Lynne F. "Laughter Is not only Medicine, It's a Management Tool." *Jaycees Magazine.* Aug./Sept. 1987: 10–11.

McMorris, Robert F., Sandra L. Urbach, and Michael C. Connor. "Effects of Incorporating Humor in Test Items." *Journal of Educational Measurement.* Summer 1985: 147–155.

Mitchell-Dwyer, Barbi. "'Are We Gonna Do Anything Fun?'" *English Journal.* Oct. 1981: 24–25.

"Nonsense." *The Creative Child and Adult Quarterly.* Autumn 1979.

Pierce, Ronald L. "Teachers and Stress: How to Cope." Council for Exceptional Children State Convention. March 1, 1990.

Rogers, Vincent R. "Laughing with Children." *Educational Leadership.* April 1984: 46–50.

Sluder, Alice Wilde. "Children and Laughter: the Elementary School Counselor's Role." *Elementary School Guidance and Counseling.* Dec. 1986: 120–127.

Sudol, David. "Dangers of Classroom Humor." *English Journal.* Oct. 1981: 26–28.

Sverdlove, Jill. "Dinner Drama." *Denver Post.* June 28, 1992.

"Teaching with Humor: A Performing Art." *Contemporary Education.* Spring 1982: 150–154.

"A Touch of Humor. " *NASSP Bulletin.* Oct. 1981.

Warnock, Peter. "Humor as a Didactic Tool in Adult Education." *Lifelong Learning: An Omnibus of Practice and Research.* 12 (1989): 22–24.

Ziv, Avner. "The Effect of Humor on Aggression Catharsis in the Classroom." *The Journal of Psychology.* 121 (1987): 359–364.

The authors

Elaine Lundberg enjoys life as a humor therapist, presenting workshops all over the country on how to effectively incorporate positive humor into personal and professional life. A former teacher at the elementary, secondary and college levels, she lives in Pennsylvania. She says her life is complete after writing this book, performing stand-up comedy and having a great son, David, who thinks she is funny. Really, really funny.

For more information about Elaine Lundberg's presentations, call her at (610) 696-2036.

Cheryl Miller Thurston is a writer who lives in Colorado with her husband Ed and the best cat in the world, Cassie. A former teacher with over 13 years of experience in the classroom, she has published many books for teachers, as well as numerous articles and plays. Her most recent project is founding Closet Accordion Players of America, a national organization that uses humor to eliminate "accordion abuse" in America.

The artist

Patricia Howard has been drawing cartoons since high school ("for quite a few years, in other words," she says). For over eight years, she designed award-winning T-shirts for her own mail-order business, Howard Graphics. She is currently an illustrator and a fine artist who specializes in portraits and florals. She lives in Durango, Colorado, with her husband Alan and her sons.

To order more copies of
If They're Laughing, They're Not Killing Each Other

Please send me _____ copies of *If They're Laughing, They're Not Killing Each Other.* I have enclosed $12.95, plus $2.50 shipping, for each book ordered. (Colorado residents, please add 39¢ sales tax, per book.)

Name_____

(School)_____
(Include only if using school address.)

Address _____
(Because we ship UPS, do not use a PO box for your address.)

City _____ State _____ Zip Code _____

Daytime phone number _____
(In case we need to contact you about your order)

Method of Payment:

☐Check   ☐VISA/Mastercard   ☐Purchase Order *(Please attach.)*

Credit Card # _____Expiration Date _____

Signature _____

Send order to:

Cottonwood Press, Inc.
305 West Magnolia, Suite 398
Fort Collins, Colorado 80521

1-800-864-4297
Call for a free catalog of practical materials for English
and language arts teachers, grades 5-12.